Solving the Retirement Mystery

Transform Your Dreams into Reality

BRADLEY FORD
Vineyard Financial

Bradley Ford | Vineyard Financial
20 NW 3rd St., Suite 300, Evansville, Indiana, 47708

Book layout ©2022 Advisors Excel, LLC

Solving the Retirement Mystery: Transform Your Dreams into Reality/Bradley Ford.

ISBN 9798300517298

Bradley Ford is registered as an Investment Advisor Representative and is a licensed insurance agent in the state of Indiana. Vineyard Financial is an independent financial services firm that helps individuals create retirement strategies using a variety of investment and insurance products to custom suit their needs and objectives.

Securities and advisory services offered only by duly registered individuals of Madison Avenue Securities, LLC (MAS), member FINRA/SIPC and a registered investment advisor. Vineyard Financial and MAS are not affiliated entities.

Insurance products are offered through the insurance business Vineyard Financial. VINEYARD FINANCIAL is also an Investment Advisory practice that offers products and services through AE Wealth Management, LLC (AEWM), a Registered Investment Adviser. AEWM does not offer insurance products. The insurance products offered by Bradley Ford are not subject to Investment Adviser requirements. AEWM and Bradley Ford are not affiliated companies.

The contents of this book are provided for informational purposes only and are not intended to serve as the basis for any financial decisions. Any tax, legal, or estate planning information is general in nature. Please remember that converting an employer plan account to a Roth IRA is a taxable event. Increased taxable income from the Roth IRA conversion may have several consequences. Be sure to consult with a qualified tax advisor before making any decisions regarding your IRA. It should not be construed as legal or tax advice. Always consult an attorney or tax professional regarding the applicability of this information to your unique situation.

Information presented is believed to be factual and up-to-date, but we do not guarantee its accuracy, and it should not be regarded as a complete analysis of the subjects discussed. All expressions of opinion are those of the author as of the date of publication and are subject to change. Content should not be construed as personalized investment advice nor should it be interpreted as an offer to buy or sell any securities mentioned. A financial advisor should be consulted before implementing any of the strategies presented.

Investing involves risk, including the potential loss of principal. No investment strategy can guarantee a profit or protect against loss in periods of declining values. Any references to protection benefits or guaranteed/lifetime income streams refer only to fixed insurance products, not securities or investment products. Annuity guarantees rely on financial strength and claims-paying ability of issuing insurance company. Annuities are insurance products that may be subject to fees, surrender charges, and holding periods, which vary by carrier. Annuities are not FDIC insured.

Any names used in the examples in this book are hypothetical only and do not represent actual clients. Vineyard Financial is not affiliated with the U.S. government or any governmental agency.

"You don't have enough faith," Jesus told them. "I tell you the truth, if you had faith even as small as a mustard seed, you could say to this mountain, 'move from here to there,' and it would move. Nothing would be impossible."

~ Matthew 17: 20

I'd like to dedicate this to all my clients, including family and friends, who have entrusted me with their futures. Also, to future clients who, perhaps after reading this, will allow me to help them live their dreams.

Table of Contents

The Importance of Planning

I f I were to meet you on an elevator and you asked for my twenty-second business pitch between floors, my answer would be simple.

My team and I will help you create your own unique, Sustainable Retirement Plan by getting your financial ducks in a row so you can have the confidence to retire, stay retired, and — more importantly — maintain your standard of living as long as you live.

The process is a four-step planning process. It's a simple process that involves you every step of the way so you can have the confidence that you can achieve your goals and dreams. Remember, dreams are just dreams until you make a plan and take action.

It's a system I've honed through decades of work with clients and more informally with family members, including my own parents.

They're good examples of how I've learned that each person has his or her own needs and comfort levels.

For instance, my mother loved my advice. She embraced it and was proud of me.

My father appreciated it, too, but my dad — one of fifteen children — was conservative in his upbringing. I once invested $15,000 for him and made reasonable rates of return, but he viewed that as me putting his money at risk, and I never heard the end of it.

However, at another point when he was about fifty-five, he asked me to review his documents, and I told him that with the assets he had, I thought he'd be smart to start taking retirement and find something else to do.

That's what he did, and he was able to volunteer as superintendent for a Lutheran cemetery for almost a decade. He got everything in order there, and he took a lot of pride in that.

My parents are the ones who taught me right and wrong, and they taught me a good work ethic. They never quite understood my entrepreneurial drive, though. I was business-minded from the get-go.

When I was growing up in Evansville, I wanted a new bike, so my mom showed me how to plant seeds. I then went door to door selling plants to people to raise the money to buy my new bike.

In college, I focused on marketing and business, but then I saw an opportunity to become a disc jockey around 1979. And, I must confess, I brought disco into Evansville. Please forgive me.

I was making $100,000 a year spinning records for about four years until a lot of others got into the business. Oh, well, it was time to grow up anyway.

As a driven person and independent thinker, I knew I was destined to have my own firm.

Back when I started in financial planning, the industry wasn't as formal as it is today. It was in its infancy, and a lot of it was insurance-based and bank-based with no software programs to do formal retirement planning. There weren't even certain licenses back then that exist today.

I trademarked the Christian-based Vineyard Financial and set about putting clients first. Just as I don't like being told what to do, I established a system that wouldn't be overbearing or overwhelming to anyone. I want people to work with us because we're good, and we listen to them.

That's how I came to create our team's four-step process, which is an organizational process where each step builds on the others.

The first step is what I call the Living Your Dream consultation. We kind of model our practice after a doctor's office. You come in, and we get to know you through a set series of questions to learn about you and your goals.

We also ask you to bring all your documents. We're trying to look for cracks in the foundation that may cause you problems down the road.

Much like when you see a doctor, we'll share information with you, but then it's up to you to take action.

We'll then set a second appointment, which is a meeting for Your Retirement Plan. These two meetings are complimentary.

Between those appointments, we'll run various scenarios. A lot of planners use a model of what will happen with 2 percent inflation. We try to be safe and look at 3 percent inflation. We examine how you're investing, and we study the tax implications of your investments.

Another key area is determining your risk comfort on a scale of 100. We run risk assessments on your investments. We believe 100 minus your age is the most you should have at risk.

Couples, of course, don't always agree on risk, so we run separate risk assessments and sometimes invest accounts differently based on the results.

This also is when we evaluate your current plans, meaning when you think you're going to be able to retire and how much you think you'll be able to spend during retirement.

Frankly, most of the time, the plans people already have fail, and we ask them how they feel about what we've discovered. Usually, we find at least three things to improve. Often, we discover a tax time bomb. We look for areas to show where we can add value, and we end by asking if you want our help.

If you do want our help, the next step is to fine tune your plan to create your own unique Sustainable Retirement Plan. That includes looking at things from a tax efficiency standpoint to determine the best time for you to take Social Security, your pensions, and your investments.

We are extremely specific with you as to how you withdraw your money because that makes a difference on your taxes. A lot of times, we show clients how they could have converted to a Roth IRA in order to pay taxes now instead of in the future.

It takes time to complete a Social Security analysis, a retirement plan, an income plan, and a tax analysis, but it's also what makes our firm special and our plan for you sound.

The final step of our process is a Service Planning Session during which we bring in other professionals, such as a CPA or an attorney, if you need help with things such as writing a will and identifying tax savings. We arrange these meetings with other professionals and then follow up to ensure everything gets done. We also introduce you to your Vineyard Financial team.

Procrastination is part of the human condition. We get it. We're human, too.

It's never too late to plan, but obviously, the sooner you can do it, the better.

Remember, all that will be there when you get there is what you send ahead.

There are all kinds of analogies to help demonstrate the need for proper financial planning with the right help.

Perhaps the simplest way to think about it is with a sports team. There may be a heck of a lot of great players on that team, but how do they all work together? Where are the deficiencies? How can they work as one to create the best winning strategy? That's where a coach comes in.

Or think of a road trip. Doesn't a map help get you there? You may think you know the way, but what if a bridge up ahead is suddenly out? How will you know how to make adjustments?

This book is about showing you how we can provide guidance. It's a working reference to my team's own winning strategy. The information can seem like a lot, but that's where we, as coaches, then come in to help.

Potential Risks to Your Ideal Retirement

Ever feel like life gets in the way and prevents you from doing things you shouldn't ignore? I think if we're honest with ourselves, we've all put off obligations we know are important. In your case, you may be reading this book because it's time to get serious about financial planning and, specifically, devising a way to ideally prepare for retirement. A retirement plan should be based on more components than just your investments or your finances. The preparation of that strategy begins with your desires, ambitions, and goals for this fulfilling season of life.

There's no such thing as a silly question — not when one of the most common questions we hear from folks regarding retirement is, "Am I going to be okay?" It often seems people are reluctant to meet with financial professionals because they worry they might sound uneducated. However, it's understandable for you to be a novice when it comes to financial issues and retirement concerns. You've been busy with your lives and your careers. Time spent away from work has meant time spent being around those you love and engaging in the activities you enjoy. Retirement provides the opportunity to do even more of that, while not fretting over work obligations.

Concerns people have about what they may encounter during retirement can be far-reaching and still perfectly legitimate. For a quick snapshot, I want to provide a brief sampling of wide-ranging issues that can come up during discussions about what to potentially brace for in retirement. This book will touch on many of these issues in further detail.

Politics: A presidential election often stirs emotions regarding potential effects on the economy. Investors grow anxious about how a new president can influence market returns. It's Congress, however, that establishes tax laws and passes spending bills. Yet the president can indirectly affect the economy and the stock market in various ways such as the appointment of policymakers, development of international relations, and influential sway on new legislation.

Taxes: An example of a president's influence can be cited in signature legislation passed during Donald Trump's first presidency, the Tax Cuts and Jobs Act of 2017, and another tax measure during his second presidency, the One Big Beautiful Bill Act. However, our tax system remains progressive, so the more you earn, the higher the tax rate within each tax bracket of subsequently higher income. A thorough understanding of tax regulations can be crucial. A financial professional can help identify potential issues a tax professional can help solve.

Inflation: General increases in the prices of goods and services, often measured using the consumer price index (CPI) often stem from fluctuations in real demand for goods and services. Inflation can discourage investment, as well as shortages in goods. A retiree's income can be impacted by the effect inflation can have on a fixed budget. The value of currency decreases because inflation erodes purchasing power.

Cybersecurity: Think you'll give up your smartphone in retirement? No way, right? It's here to stay, along with other intellectual gadgetry, including devices that have not been patented or invented yet. Retirees are becoming more tech-savvy, yet they can also be more trusting, which can be problematic when responding to potential scammers by phone, text, or email. Cybercrime often uses technology to target potential victims. Scammers, much like technology, figure to only grow more sophisticated over time.

CHAPTER 1

Longevity

Y ou would think the prospect of the grave would loom more frightening as we age, yet many retirees say their number one concern is actually running out of money in their twilight years.[1] Unfortunately, this concern is justified because of one significant factor: We're living longer.

According to the Social Security Administration's 2011 Trustee Report, in 1950, the average life expectancy for a sixty-five-year-old man was seventy-eight, and the average for a sixty-five-year-old woman was eighty-one.[2] In the 2023 Trustees Report issued by the SSA, those averages were eighty-three and eighty-six, respectively.[3]

The bottom line of many retirees' budget woes comes down to this: They just didn't plan to live so long. Now, when we are younger and in our working years, that's not something we necessarily see as a bad thing; don't some people fantasize about living forever or, at least, reaching the ripe old age of 100?

However, with a longer lifespan, we face a few snags as we retire. Our resources are finite — we only have so much money

---

[1] Brett Arends. MarketWatch. June 5, 2023. "Americans are 'more afraid of running out of money than death'"
https://www.marketwatch.com/story/americans-are-more-afraid-of-running-out-money-than-death-ee5e22e9
[2] Social Security Administration. 2024. "Actuarial Publications: Cohort Life Expectancy" https://www.ssa.gov/oact/TR/2011/lr5a4.html
[3] Social Security Administration. 2023. "Period Life Expectancy — 2023 OASDI Trustees Report" https://www.ssa.gov/OACT/TR/2023/lr5a4.html

to provide income — but our lifespans can be unpredictably long, perhaps longer than our resources allow. Also, longer lives don't necessarily equate with healthier lives. The longer you live, the more money you will likely need to spend on health care, even excluding long-term care needs like nursing homes.

You will also run into inflation. If you don't plan to live another twenty-five years but end up doing so, inflation at an average of 3 percent will approximately double the price of goods over that time period.

Because we don't necessarily get to have our cake and eat it, too, our collective increased longevity hasn't necessarily increased the healthy years of our lives. Typically, our life-extending care most widely applies to the time in our lives when we will need more care in general. Think of common situations like a pacemaker at eighty-five, or cancer treatment at seventy-eight.

"Wow, Brad," I can hear you say. "Way to start with the good news first."

I know, I've painted a grim picture, but all I'm concerned about here is cost. It's hard to put a dollar sign on life, but that is essentially what we're talking about when discussing longevity and finances. Living longer isn't a bad thing; it just costs more, and one key to a sound retirement strategy is preparing for it in advance.

Imagine having a jigsaw puzzle with 100 pieces, but you do not know how to begin putting it together.

A lot of times, people have the necessary pieces to retire, but they don't know how to put them together and test when that can happen.

You may be surprised to learn you can retire now.

Imagine someone with health issues learning that good news.

Sometimes, people discover they can immediately reduce their stress and start enjoying time off. They can begin to travel and do the things they always wanted to do because they have confidence the income they have will last their lifetimes.

We plan for the ups and downs of investments and create accounts that can be used to provide income regardless of what the market is doing.

We help reduce taxes you pay during retirement, too, by being intentional as to which types of accounts will be used for income, depending on tax rates at that time, and whether it might make sense each year to implement other tax-saving strategies such as Roth conversions, which help give more control over taxes now and in the future.

Living longer may be more expensive, but it can be so meaningful when you plan for your "just-in-cases."

Retiring Early

A key part of planning for retirement revolves around retirement income. After all, retirement is cutting the cord that tethers you to your employer — and your monthly check. However, that check often comes with many other benefits, particularly health care. Health care is often the thing that can unexpectedly put dreams for an early retirement on hold. Some employers offer health benefits to their retired workers, but that number has declined drastically over the past several decades.

In 1988, among employers who offered health benefits to their workers, 66 percent offered health benefits to their retirees. That number has since dwindled to 21 percent.[4] So, with employer-offered retirement health benefits on the wane, this becomes a major point of concern for anyone who is looking to retire, particularly those who are looking to retire before age sixty-five, when they would become eligible for Medicare coverage.

Fidelity estimates that the average retired couple at age sixty-five will need approximately $315,000 for health care

---

4 Henry J. Kaiser Family Foundation. October 27, 2022. "2022 Employer Health Benefits Survey" https://www.kff.org/report-section/ehbs-2022-section-11-retiree-health-benefits/

expenses in retirement, not including long-term care.[5] Do you think it's likely that cost will decrease?

Even if you are working until age sixty-five or have plans to cover your health expenses until that point, I often have clients who incorrectly assume Medicare is their golden ticket to cover all expenses. That is simply not the case.

Retiring Later

Planning for a long life in retirement partly depends on when you retire. While many people end up retiring earlier than they anticipated — due to injuries, layoffs, family crises, and other unforeseen circumstances — continuing to work past age sixty (and even sixty-five) is still a viable option for others and can be an excellent way to help establish financial confidence in retirement.

There are many reasons for this. For one, you obviously still earn a paycheck and the benefits accompanying it. Medical coverage and beefing up your retirement accounts with further savings can be significant by themselves, but continuing to generate income should also keep you from dipping into your retirement funds, further allowing them the opportunity to grow.

Additionally, for many workers, their nine-to-five job is more than just clocking in and out. Having a sense of purpose can keep us active physically, mentally, and socially. That kind of activity and level of engagement may also help stave off many of the health problems that plague retirees. Avoiding a sedentary life is one of the advantages of staying plugged into the workforce, if possible.

Some people are smart enough to plan financially for their retirement but don't think about what they'll do in retirement.

---

[5] Fidelity. June 21, 2023. "How to plan for rising health care costs" https://www.fidelity.com/viewpoints/personal-finance/plan-for-rising-health-care-costs

I know of someone who gained weight almost immediately after he retired and didn't look or sound as healthy as he had before retiring.

It wasn't until he created a plan for his retirement that he was back to his old self.

His experience is what made me realize I need to help coach clients to map out not just their financial futures but also their to-do plans for retirement.

Your go-go years usually last into your mid-seventies.

Next, come your slow-go years. Here, your quality of life isn't quite as good, and you have more money going toward medical expenses.

Finally, there are your no-go years when you're not able to do as much. That's often your mid-to-late eighties. I saw my parents reach that age. They had money but couldn't spend it.

Your goal should be not just to retire but to have a plan for how you'll spend your money along the way. You don't want to get to your no-go years and realize you could have been enjoying your money more.

Health Care

Take a second to reflect on your health care plan. Although working up to or even past age sixty-five could allow you to avoid a coverage gap between your working years and Medicare, that may not be an option for you. Even if it is, when you retire, you will need to make some decisions about what kind of insurance coverage you may need to supplement your Medicare. Are there any medical needs you have that may require coverage in addition to Medicare? Did your parents or grandparents have any inherited medical conditions you might consider using a special savings plan to cover?

These are all questions that are important to review with your financial professional so you can be sure you have enough money put aside for health care.

Long-Term Care

Longevity means the need for long-term care is statistically more likely to happen. If you intend to pass on a legacy, planning for long-term care is paramount, since most estimates project nearly 70 percent of Americans who reach age sixty-five will need some type of it.[6] However, this may be one of the biggest, most stressful pieces of longevity planning I encounter in my work. For one thing, who wants to talk about the point in their lives when they may feel the most limited? Who wants to dwell on what will happen if they can no longer toilet, bathe, dress, or feed themselves?

I get it; this is a less-than-fun part of planning. But a little bit of preparation now can go a long way!

When it comes to your longevity, just like with your goals, one of the important things to do is sit and dream. It may not be the fun, road-trip-to-the-Grand-Canyon kind of dreaming, but you can spend time envisioning how you want your twilight years to look.

For instance, if it is important for you to live in your home for as long as possible, who will provide for the day-to-day fixes and to-dos of housework if you become ill? Will you set aside money for a service, or do you have relatives or friends nearby whom you could comfortably allow to help you? Do you prefer in-home care over a nursing home or assisted living? This could be a good time to discuss the possibility of moving into a retirement community versus staying where you are or whether it's worth moving to another state and leaving relatives behind.

These are all important factors to discuss with your spouse and children, as *now* is the right time to address questions and concerns. For instance, is aging in place more important to one spouse than the other? Are the friends or relatives who live

---

[6] Claire Samuels. A Place for Mom. September 13, 2023. "Long-Term Care Statistics: A Portrait of Americans in Assisted Living, Nursing Homes, and Skilled Nursing Facilities" https://www.aplaceformom.com/senior-living-data/articles/long-term-care-statistics

nearby emotionally, physically, and financially capable of helping you for a time if you face an illness?

Many families I meet with find these conversations very uncomfortable, particularly when children discuss nursing home care with their parents. A knee-jerk reaction for many is to promise they will care for their aging parents. This is noble and well-intentioned, but there needs to be an element of realism here. Does "help" from an adult child mean they stop by and help you with laundry, cooking, home maintenance, and bills? Or does it mean they move you into their spare room when you have hip surgery? Are they prepared to help you use the restroom and bathe if that becomes difficult for you to do on your own?

I don't mean to discourage families from caring for their own; this can be a profoundly admirable relationship when it works out. However, I've seen families put off planning for late-in-life care based on a tenuous promise that the adult children would care for their parents, only to watch as the support system crumbles. Sometimes, this is because the assumed caregiver hasn't given serious thought to the preparation they would need, both in a formal sense and regarding their personal physical, emotional, and financial commitments. This is often also because we can't see the future: Alzheimer's disease and other maladies of old age can exact a heavy toll. When a loved one reaches the point where they are at risk of wandering away or need help with two or more activities of daily living, it can be more than one person or a family can realistically handle.

If you know what you want, communicate with your family about both the best-case and worst-case scenarios. Then, hope for the best, and plan for the worst.

Realistic Cost of Care

Included in your planning should be a consideration for the cost of long-term care. The potential costs for such care and treatment can be underestimated, especially by those who have maintained robust health and find it difficult to envision future declines in their condition.

Another piece of planning for long-term care costs is anticipating inflation. It's common knowledge that prices have been and keep rising, which can lower your purchasing power on everything from food to medical care. Long-term care is a big piece of the inflation-disparity pie.

While local costs vary from state to state, the following table shows the national median for various forms of long-term care (plus projections that account for a 3 percent annual inflation, so you can see what I am referencing):[7]

Long-Term Care Costs: Inflation				
	Informal Care	Home Care	Assisted Living	Nursing Home (semi-private room)
Annual 2025	$43,299	$39,749	$67,085	$109,628
Annual 2035	$58,190	$53,420	$90,157	$154,641
Annual 2045	$78,202	$71,791	$121,163	$218,137
Annual 2054	$102,036	$93,672	$158,090	$297,298

Fund Your Long-Term Care

One common mistake I see occurs in those who haven't planned for long-term care because they assume the government will

---

[7] Nationwide. 2024. "Compare Long-term Care costs from state to state" https://nationwidefinancialltcmap.hvsfinancial.com/

provide everything. But that's a big misconception. The government has two health insurance programs: Medicare and Medicaid. These can greatly assist you in your health care *needs* in retirement but usually don't provide enough coverage to cover all your health care *costs* in retirement. My firm isn't a government outpost, so we don't get to make decisions regarding policy and specifics about either of these programs. I'm going to give an overview of both, but if you want to dive into the details of these programs, you can visit www.Medicare.gov and www.Medicaid.gov.

Medicare

Medicare covers those aged sixty-five and older and those who are disabled. Medicare's coverage of any nursing-home-related health issues is limited. It might cover your nursing home stay if it is not a "custodial" stay and isn't long-term. For example, if you break a bone or suffer a stroke, stay in a nursing home for rehabilitative care, and then return home, Medicare may cover you. However, if you have developed dementia or are looking to move to a nursing facility because you can no longer bathe, dress, toilet, feed yourself, or take care of your hygiene, etc., then Medicare is not going to pay for your nursing home costs.[8]

You can enroll in Medicare anytime during the three months before and three months after your sixty-fifth birthday. Miss your enrollment deadline, and you could risk paying increased premiums for the rest of your life.[9] On top of prompt enrollment, there are a few other things to think about when it comes to Medicare, not least among them being the need to understand the different "parts," what they do, and what they don't cover.

---

[8] Medicare. 2024. "What Part A covers" https://www.medicare.gov/what-medicare-covers/what-part-a-covers

[9] Medicare. 2024. "When can I sign up for Medicare?" https://www.medicare.gov/basics/get-started-with-medicare/sign-up/when-can-i-sign-up-for-medicare

Part A

Medicare Part A is what you might think of as "classic" Medicare. Hospital care, some types of home health care, and major medical care fall under this. While most enrollees pay nothing for this service (as they likely paid into the system for at least ten years), you might have to, based on either work history or delayed signup. In 2025, a hospital stay does have a deductible — $1,676[10] Also, if you have a hospital stay surpassing sixty days, you could be looking at additional costs. Keep in mind, Medicare doesn't pay for long-term care and services.

Part B

Medicare Part B is an essential piece of wrap-around coverage for Medicare Part A. It helps pay for doctor visits and outpatient services. This also comes with a price tag: Although the Part B annual deductible is only $257 in 2025, you will still pay 20 percent of all costs after that, with no limit on out-of-pocket expenses. The Part B monthly premium for 2025 ranges from the standard amount of $185 to $594.[11]

Part C

Medicare Part C (more commonly known as a Medicare Advantage plan) is an alternative to a combination of Parts A, B, and sometimes D. Administered through private insurance companies, these have a variety of costs and restrictions, and they are subject to the specific policies and rules of the issuing carrier.

---

[10] Centers for Medicare & Medicaid Services. November 8, 2024. "2025 Medicare Parts A&B Premiums and Deductibles"
https://www.cms.gov/newsroom/fact-sheets/2025-medicare-parts-b-premiums-and-deductibles
[11] Ibid.

Part D

Medicare Part D is also offered through a private insurer and is supplemental to Parts A and B, as its primary purpose is to cover prescription drugs. Like any private insurance plan, Part D has its quirks and rules that vary from insurer to insurer.

The base Part D beneficiary premium is $36.78 in 2025.[12] The Inflation Reduction Act passed in 2022 caps annual prescription drug costs to $2000 as part of Medicare Part D coverage. Previously, Americans on Part D private drug insurance adhered to a coverage gap named the Donut Hole. The coverage gap allowance in the Donut Hole forced Americans to pay up to 25 percent out of pocket for all covered medications. The Donut Hole no longer exists.

If drug costs reach the $2,000 gap, you do not have to pay a copayment or coinsurance for Part D drugs for the remainder of the calendar year. You can also spread your drug costs into monthly payments throughout the year.

Medicare Supplements

Medicare Supplement Insurance, MedSupp, Medigap, or plans labeled Medicare Part F, G, H, I, J ... Known by a variety of monikers, this is just a fancy way of saying "medical coverage for those over sixty-five that picks up the tab for whatever the federal Medicare program(s) doesn't." Again, costs, limitations, etc., vary by carrier.

Does that sound like a bunch of government alphabet soup to you? It certainly does to me. And did you read the fine print? Unpredictable costs, varied restrictions, difficult-to-compare benefits, donut holes, and coverage gaps. That's par for the course with health care plans throughout our adult lives. What gives? I thought Medicare was supposed to be easier, comprehensive, and at no cost!

12 Shawn Radcliffe. Healthline. November 12, 2024. "5 Changes to Medicare in 2025 Will Affect Part D Coverage, Drug Costs" https://www.healthline.com/health-news/medicare-part-d-2025-changes-drug-costs-plan-coverage

The truth is there is probably no stage of life when health care is easy to understand.

Many people don't retire before sixty-five because they don't think they can get health care, but options are available for substantially subsidized health care.

Having guidance is the key to figuring out what's available or, if you're of age to take Medicare, which plan you should choose.

One of the best things you can do for yourself is to scope out the health care field early, compare costs often, and prepare for out-of-pocket costs well in advance — decades, if possible.

Medicaid

Medicaid is a program the states administer, so funding, protocol, and limitations vary. Compared to Medicare, Medicaid more widely covers nursing home care, but it targets a different demographic: those with low incomes.

If you have more assets than the Medicaid limit in your state and need nursing home care, you will need to use those assets to pay for your care. You will also have a list of additional state-approved ways to use or spend some of these assets over the Medicaid limit, such as pre-purchasing burial plots and funeral expenses or paying off debts. After that, your remaining assets fund your nursing home stay until they are gone, at which point Medicaid will jump in.

Some people aren't stymied by this, thinking they will just pass on their financial assets early by gifting them to relatives, friends, and causes so they can qualify for Medicaid when they need it. However, to prevent this exact scenario, Uncle Sam has implemented what's called the "look-back period." Currently, if you enroll in Medicaid, you are subject to having the government scrutinize the last five years of your finances for large gifts or expenses that may subject you to penalties, temporarily making you ineligible for Medicaid coverage.

Provisions in the One Big Beautiful Bill Act (OBBBA) enacted in 2025 included significant changes to Medicaid. Changes primarily focused on eligibility and funding, with potential implications for millions of Americans. The bill mandates work requirements for able-bodied adults aged nineteen through sixty-four, increases redetermination frequency, and limits state-directed Medicaid managed care payments. New requirements will be phased in, starting in 2026.[13]

So, if you're planning to preserve your money for future generations and retain control of your financial resources during your lifetime, you'll probably want to prepare for the costs of longevity beyond a "government plan."

Self-Funding

One way to fund a longer life is the old-fashioned way, through self-funding. There are a variety of financial tools you can use, and they all have their pros and cons. If your assets are in low-interest financial vehicles (savings, bonds, CDs), you risk letting inflation erode the value of your dollar. If you are relying on the stock market, you have more growth potential, but you'll also want to consider the possible implications of market volatility. What if your assets take a hit? If you suffer a loss in your retirement portfolio in early or mid-retirement, you might have the option to "tighten your belt," so to speak, and cut back on discretionary spending to allow your portfolio the room to bounce back. But if you are retired and depend on income from a stock account that just hit a downward stride, what are you going to do?

Health Savings Accounts

These days, you might also be able to self-fund through a health savings account (HSA) if you have access to one through a high-deductible health plan (you will not qualify to save in an HSA after enrolling in Medicare).

---

[13] Center for Medicare Advocacy. July 24, 2025. "Impact of the "Big Bill" on Medicare" https://medicareadvocacy.org/impact-of-the-big-bill-on-medicare/

Also, under the tax bill signed in July 2025, if your health plan is Bronze-level or you use direct primary care, you might be newly eligible to open and fund an HSA — even if you weren't eligible before.[14] If you qualify for an HSA, you can make a one-time move from your IRA into your HSA (up to the annual limit). That money becomes tax-free if used for future qualified medical expenses.[15]

In an HSA, any growth of your tax-deductible contributions will be tax-free, and any distributions paid out for qualified health costs are also tax-free. Long-term care expenses count as health costs, so if this is an option available to you, it is one way to use the tax advantages to self-fund your longevity. Bear in mind if you are younger than sixty-five, any money you use for non-qualified expenses will be subject to taxes and penalties, and if you are older than sixty-five, any HSA money you use for non-medical expenses is subject to income tax.

LTCI

Now, there are a few oft-cited components of LTCI that make it unattractive for some:

- Expense — LTCI can be expensive. It is generally less expensive the younger you are, but a sixty-five-year-old man would pay about $2,749 annually for a $4,000 monthly benefit and 3-year benefit period with a 3% lifetime inflation protection rider, while a woman that age would pay about $4,599 annually for a similar policy, assuming standard rates.[16] And the annual cost typically increases from there the older you are.

---

[14] Chase Charaba. Remodel health. August 6, 2025. "What healthcare changes are in the One Big Beautiful Bill Act (OBBBA).
https://remodelhealth.com/what-healthcare-changes-are-in-obbba/
[15] Fidelity. May 13, 2025. "IRA-to-HSA rollovers"
https://www.fidelity.com/learning-center/smart-money/ira-to-hsa-rollover
[16] Joshua Rodriguez. CBS News. May 1, 2024. "How much does long-term care insurance cost for a 65-year-old?"
https://www.cbsnews.com/news/how-much-does-long-term-care-insurance-cost-for-a-65-year-old/

- Limited options — LTCI may be expensive for consumers, but it can also be expensive for companies that offer it. With fewer companies willing to take on that expense, the market narrows, limiting opportunities to price shop for policies with different options or custom benefits.
- If you know you need it, you might not be able to get it — Insurance companies offering LTCI are taking on a risk that you may need LTCI. That risk is the foundation of the product — you may or may not need it. If you know you will need it because you have a dementia diagnosis or another illness for which you will need long-term care, you will likely not qualify for LTCI coverage.
- Use it or lose it — If you have LTCI and are in the minority of Americans who die having never needed long-term care, all the money you paid into your LTCI policy is gone.
- Possibly fluctuating rates — Your premium rate is not locked in on LTCI. Companies maintain the ability to raise or lower your premium amounts. This means some seniors face an ultimatum: Keep funding a policy at what might be a less affordable rate *or* lose coverage and let go of all the money they have paid so far.

After that, you might be thinking, "How can people possibly be interested in LTCI?" But let me repeat myself — it's anticipated that as many as 70 percent of Americans will need long-term care. And although only one in ten Americans aged fifty-five-plus has purchased LTCI, keep in mind the high cost of nursing home care. Can you afford $7,000 a month to put into nursing home care and still have enough left over to help protect your legacy?

This is a genuine concern, which is underscored by a 2024 report released by the Alzheimer's Association. It stipulates that 6.1 percent of Americans aged sixty-five and over suffered from Alzheimer's disease in 2020. It projects that 13.8 percent of Americans in that age group will be affected by the disease in 2050. It's worth noting that baby boomers, a generation born from 1948-64, will all turn sixty-five by 2030.[17] So, not to sound like a broken record, but it is vitally important to have a plan in place to deal with longevity and long-term care, especially if you intend to leave a financial legacy.

I absolutely recommend long-term care insurance because I know what life can be like without it.

It's projected that in addition to regular medical costs, healthy people in retirement will spend approximately $5.700 per person ($11,400 for married couples) annually on health care after turning sixty-five.[18]

It's hard to think about, but at some stage, you may get to a point where you can't get in and out of bed on your own or even feed yourself. Or you may be cognitively impaired.

Good long-term care coverage will pay to help, but individuals need a clear understanding of what they're buying and what's included and excluded.

Sometimes, there are other options for coverage, such as using old life insurance policy annuities and combining them into a new policy.

Whatever the solution, it's key to think about it while you're still in good health. Otherwise, the later years can be pretty sad.

A few relevant statistics to keep in mind:

- The longer you live, the more health care you will likely need to pay for.
- The median cost of a private nursing home room in the United States between 2022 and 2023 was $9,034 a month.[19] But keep in mind that is just the nursing home

[17] Alzheimer's Association. 2024. "Alzheimer's Disease Facts and Figures" Page 32. https://www.alz.org/alzheimers-dementia/facts-figures

[18] RBC Wealth Management. 2024. "The real cost of health care in retirement" https://www.rbcwealthmanagement.com/en-us/insights/the-real-cost-of-health-care-in-retirement#

[19] Merritt Whitley. A Place for Mom. May 19, 2023. "How Much Do Nursing Homes Cost? A State-By-State Guide" https://www.aplaceformom.com/caregiver-resources/articles/nursing-homes-cost

— it doesn't include other medical costs, let alone pleasantries like entertainment or hobby spending.

- As referenced earlier, Fidelity calculated in a 2022 study that a healthy couple retiring at age sixty-five could expect to pay around $315,000 over the course of retirement to cover health and medical expenses.[20]

I know. "Whoa, there, Brad, I was hoping to have a realistic idea of health costs, not be driven over by a cement mixer!"

The good news is, while we don't know these exact costs in advance, we know there *will* be costs. And you won't have to pay your total Medicare lifetime premiums in one day as a lump sum. Now that you have a good idea of health care costs in retirement, you can *plan* for them! That's the real point here: Planning in advance can keep you from feeling nickel-and-dimed to your wits' end. Instead, having a sizeable portion of your assets earmarked for health care can allow you the freedom to choose health care networks, coverage options, and long-term care possibilities that you like.

Product Riders

LTCI and self-funding are not the only ways to plan for the expenses of longevity. Some companies are getting creative with their products, particularly insurance companies. One way they are retooling to meet people's needs is through optional product riders on annuities and life insurance. Elsewhere in this book, I talk about annuity basics, but here's a brief overview: Annuities are insurance contracts. You pay the insurance company a premium — either as a lump sum or as a series of payments over a set amount of time — in exchange for guaranteed income payments.

One of the advantages of an annuity is it has access to riders, which allow you to tweak your contract for a fee, depending on

---

[20] Fidelity. June 21, 2023. "How to plan for rising health care costs" https://www.fidelity.com/viewpoints/personal-finance/plan-for-rising-health-care-costs

the type and length of the coverage. On average, these FIA rider fees cost up to 1.25 percent annually.[21] One annuity rider some companies offer is a long-term care rider. If you have an annuity with a long-term care rider and are not in need of long-term care, your contract behaves as any annuity contract would — nothing changes. Generally speaking, if you reach a point when you can't perform multiple functions of daily life on your own, you notify the insurance company, and if you meet the long-term care rider requirements, your additional rider benefits can be activated to help you pay for your long-term care needs. An insurance company representative will turn on those provisions of your contract. Activating LTC rider benefits is more involved than simply calling your insurance carrier. A physician has to confirm that you cannot perform the required amount of activities of daily living (ADLs).

Like LTCI, different companies and products offer different options. Some annuity long-term care riders offer coverage of two years in a nursing home situation. Others cap expenses at two times the original annuity's value. It greatly depends. Some people prefer this option because there isn't a "use-it-or-lose-it" piece; if you die without ever having needed long-term care, you still will have had the income benefit from the base contract.

Still, as with any annuities or insurance contracts, there are the usual restrictions and limitations. Withdrawing money from the contract will affect future income payments, early distributions can result in a penalty, income taxes may apply, and, because the insurance company's solvency is what guarantees your payments, it's important to do your research about the insurance company you are considering purchasing a contract from.

Understandably, a discussion on long-term care is bound to feel at least a little tedious. Yet, this is an important piece of

---

[21] Shawn Plummer. The Annuity Expert. 2024. "A Guide To Annuity Fees" https://www.annuityexpertadvice.com/types-of-annuities/annuity-fees/

planning for income in retirement, particularly if you want to leave a legacy.

I know of someone who was able to retire in his fifties after confirming the combination of his pension, his Social Security, and his spouse's pension. Social Security should provide adequate supplemental retirement income for the rest of their lives. They decided their assets could provide additional benefits but eventually would most likely go to their children.

Since their income plan was more than adequate, they looked at what could disrupt that income, and one concern was the potential cost of long-term care over their extended lifetimes. They opted against using discretionary assets to buy long-term health insurance coverage. They argued that the premiums could increase as they got older, and good genetics ran in their families, so they might not need the coverage.

That decision affected their later years when the wife needed home health care and later, assisted living care. To pay for the care, the money came from their bank account. This consequently caused them to make decisions that were probably not as smart as they would have been had they bought long-term care coverage earlier.

Spousal Planning

Here's one thing to keep in mind no matter how you plan to save: Many of us will be planning for more than ourselves. Look back at all the stats on health events and the likelihood of long life and long-term care. If they hold true for a single individual, then the likelihood of having a costly health or long-term care event is even higher for a married couple. You'll be planning for not just one life, but two. So, when it comes to long-term care insurance, annuities, self-funding, or whatever strategy you are looking at using, be sure you are funding longevity for the both of you.

CHAPTER 2

Taxes

W here to begin with taxes? Perhaps by acknowledging we all bear responsibility for the resources we share, such as roads, bridges, and schools. Every American's patriotic duty is to pay their fair share of taxes. Many would agree with me. However, while they don't mind paying their fair share, they're not interested in paying one cent more than that!

Now, just talking about taxes probably takes your mind to April — tax season. You are probably thinking about all the forms you collect and how you file. Perhaps you are thinking about your certified public accountant or another qualified tax professional and saying to yourself, "I've already got taxes taken care of, thanks!"

However, what I see when people come into my office is that their relationship with their tax professional is purely a January through April relationship. That means they may have a tax *professional*, but not a tax *planner*.

What I mean is tax planning extends beyond filing taxes. In April, we are required to settle our accounts with the IRS to make sure we have paid up on our bill or even the score if we have overpaid. But real tax planning is about making each financial move in a way that allows you to keep the most money in your pocket and out of Uncle Sam's.

Now, as a caveat, I want to emphasize I am neither a CPA nor a tax preparer, but I see the way taxes affect my clients, and I

21

have plenty of experience helping clients implement tax-efficient strategies in their retirement plans in conjunction with their tax professionals.

It is especially important to me to help my clients develop tax-efficient strategies in their retirement plans because each dollar they can keep in their pockets is a dollar we can put to work.

There are tax planners and tax preparers. The planners look ahead, and the preparers have more of a rearview mirror look.

We work with tax professionals who help you look ahead and take action.

The benefit to working with these experts is they can help you find ways to avoid capital gains taxes or minimize taxes through wise Social Security decisions. They might have smart income distribution options or Roth conversion strategies. If you own a business, they likely will have business tax strategies.

Every dime spent on taxes is a dime you will never see again, and you have no control over it. So, by planning for taxes, you should have more confidence in your retirement and more control over your taxes in retirement.

Every dollar we can save you in taxes is a dollar you can spend on other things important to you.

The Fed

Now, in the United States, taxes can be a rather uncertain proposition. Depending on who is in the White House and which party controls Congress, we might be tempted to assume tax rates could either decline or increase in the next four to eight years accordingly. However, there is one (large!) factor we, as a nation, must confront: the national debt.

Currently, according to USDebtClock.org, we are over $37,000,000,000,000 in debt and climbing. That's $37 *trillion* with a "T." With just $1 trillion, you could park it in the bank at a zero percent interest rate and spend more than $54 million every day for fifty years without hitting a zero balance.

Even if Congress got a handle and stopped that debt from its daily compound, divided by each taxpayer, we each would owe about $324,000. So, will that be check, cash, or Venmo?[22]

My point here isn't to give you anxiety. I'm just cautioning you that even with the rosiest of outlooks on our personal income tax rates, none of us should count on low tax rates for the long term. Instead, you and your network of professionals (tax, legal, and financial) should constantly be looking for ways to take advantage of tax-saving opportunities as they come.

So, how can we get started?

Know Your Limits

One of the foundational pieces of tax planning is knowing and understanding your marginal tax rate. Marginal tax rate is the tax rate you pay on your highest dollar of income. In the United States, we use a progressive tax system, meaning your marginal tax rate increases as your taxable income increases. However, to be clear, not all of your income is taxed at that highest rate — only the upper portion.

A taxpayer's income is divided into tax brackets, and the brackets determine the rate applied to increments of the filer's taxable income.

For example, if your single friend tells you she is in the 22 percent tax bracket, that means her highest amount of income is taxed at 22 percent, but chunks of her income are taxed at lower rates. Using the 2025 tax bracket, her first $11,925 of income will be taxed at 10 percent, but her next chunk of income ($11,926 to $48,475) will be taxed at 12 percent. Finally, her income, beginning at $48,476, will be taxed at 22 percent. Her tax owed for the year — before any additional taxes or credits — is the accumulation of those three amounts.

---

[22] usdebtclock.org. Accessed on September 25, 2025.

2025 Tax Brackets		
Tax Rate	**Single filers**	**Married filing jointly**
10%	$0 to $11,925	Up to $23,850
12%	$11,926 to $48,475	$23,851-$96,950
22%	$48,476 to $103,350	$96,951-$206,700
24%	$103,351 to $197,300	$206,701-$394,600
32%	$197,301 to $250.525	$394,601-$501,050
35%	$250,526 to $626,350	$501,051-$751,600
37%	$626,351 or more	Over $751,600

[23]

It's important to note the difference between marginal and effective tax rates. The effective tax rate represents the percentage of taxable income an individual pays in taxes. To calculate the effective rate, divide the total dollar amount you pay in income tax by your total income. Thus, it is the average rate and is almost always a lower percentage than a marginal rate.

Why are marginal and effective rates important in retirement planning? Federal income tax is one of the biggest expenses individuals pay in their lives. In some cases, the lifetime amount can exceed lifetime mortgage payments. Although there are federal tax breaks for Americans over the age of sixty-five, many former high-income earners continue to pay income taxes. Estimating your marginal tax rate is one of the components in determining when to begin Social Security and a crucial factor regarding Roth IRA conversions. Also, a thorough analysis of current and future marginal tax rates is

---

[23] Alex Durante. Tax Foundation. "2025 Tax Brackets" https://taxfoundation.org/data/all/federal/2025-tax-brackets/

important in the strategic planning for required minimum distributions (RMDs) on tax-deferred retirement accounts.

Assuming a Lower Tax Rate

Retirement has always been imagined as a time when you stop working and no longer earn wages or self-employment income. In the past, Social Security benefits were not subject to taxation. Even though pensions were usually taxable, their income stream didn't fully replace a recipient's previous salary. If you needed to pull from your investment funds during retirement, keep in mind that the principal had already been taxed. In general, prior to the 1970s, your income during retirement — your cash inflow – was usually taxed at a lower rate than when you were working because you had less income and certain portions of it were not taxable.

In 1978, lawmakers created Section 401 of the Internal Revenue Code to prevent companies from using tax-advantaged profit-sharing plans to primarily benefit executives. However, businessman Ted Benna reimagined this code as the foundation of the modern 401(k). This innovation ultimately led to the decline of traditional company pension plans, while shifting both control and risk to employees. The most significant change was the shift of taxation from when employees were paid and when investment income was earned to the time of withdrawal. This tax advantage encouraged individuals to save more money in tax-deferred plans than they would have in regular savings accounts, up to the allowed limits.

In addition, in 1983, Social Security introduced new tax brackets to address the problem of decreasing reserves. This resulted in both the potential for Social Security to become taxable and a significant shift in retirement planning strategy. Within a five-year period, the retirement planning landscape changed for decades going forward, possibly forever.

A big selling point for qualified retirement accounts (401(k)s, 403(b)s, IRAs, etc.) is the theory that people will pay less in tax during their retirement years than during their working years when they're putting that money away. The idea is that you're allowed to "defer" paying the tax on that income until your marginal tax rate drops in retirement. Hence, you pay less in tax on that income.

But what if it doesn't pan out that way? For some retirees, their marginal tax rate will stay the same in retirement or even increase. If you have a healthy balance in your qualified retirement account, combining its RMDs or even a Roth conversion with Social Security can result in what is called the "tax torpedo." This tax increase occurs when a larger percent of your Social Security becomes taxable, and that same income increase consequently bumps a taxpayer up to a higher marginal rate.

401(k)s/IRAs/Roth IRAs

One sometimes-unexpected piece of tax planning in retirement concerns the 401(k) or IRA. Most of us have one of these accounts or an equivalent. We pay in throughout our working lives, dutifully socking away a portion of our earnings in these tax-deferred accounts. There's the rub: tax-*deferred*, not tax-*free*. Very rarely is anything free of taxation when you get down to it. Using 401(k)s and IRAs in retirement is no different. The taxes the government deferred when you were in your working years are now coming due, and you will pay taxes on that income at whatever your current tax rate is.

Just to ensure Uncle Sam gets his due, the government also has an RMD rule. Beginning at age seventy-three (or seventy-five if you were born in 1960 or after), you are required to withdraw a certain minimum amount every year from your 401(k) or IRA, or else you will face a tax penalty on any RMD monies you should have withdrawn but didn't — and that's on top of income tax. The SECURE Act 2.0 reduced the penalty to

25 percent (from 50 percent). Timely corrections also can further reduce the penalty to 10 percent.[24]

Of course, there is also the Roth account. You can think of the difference between a Roth and a traditional retirement account as the difference between taxing the seed and taxing the harvest. Because Roths get funded with post-tax dollars, there aren't tax penalties for early withdrawals of the principal, nor are there taxes on the growth after you reach age fifty-nine-and-one-half. Perhaps best of all, there are no RMDs. Of course, you must own a Roth account for a minimum of five years before you are able to take advantage of all its features.

This is one more area where it pays to be aware of your marginal tax rate. Some people may opt to put any excess RMDs from their traditional retirement accounts into stocks or insurance. Others may find it advantageous to "convert" their traditional retirement account funds to Roth account funds in a year during which they are in a lower tax bracket.

One measure in the OBBB legislation established a "Trump Account" for eligible newborn children born in the U.S. between 2025 and 2028. The federal government will deposit $1,000 into a qualified financial account. Consumers can then invest up to $5,000 per year after tax. The account grows tax-free. Withdrawals may begin when the child turns eighteen.[25]

Roth IRA Conversions

A Roth conversion simply means converting (or withdrawing) monies from your traditional, tax-deferred retirement accounts and moving them to a Roth account. Once inside the Roth, any growth on these funds will accumulate completely tax-free, and tax will not be owed when the Roth funds are withdrawn,

---

[24] Jim Probasco. Investopedia. October 20, 2023. "SECURE 2.0 Act of 2022: Overview, Rules, Limits." https://www.investopedia.com/secure-2-0-definition-5225115

[25] Fidelity. August 1, 2025. "New tax law: 4 big changes for families" https://www.fidelity.com/learning-center/personal-finance/trump-accounts-big-beautiful-bill

assuming the conditions noted above. This is an exciting opportunity for accumulation! However, a thoughtful strategy is beneficial in the conversion process. Since dollars were placed into the traditional account pre-tax and the growth is taxable in these accounts, tax is owed on *all* the money converted to the Roth. Converting an employer plan account to a Roth IRA is a taxable event. Increased taxable income from the Roth IRA conversion may have several consequences, including (but not limited to) a need for additional tax withholding or estimated tax payments, the loss of certain tax deductions and credits, higher taxes on Social Security benefits, and higher Medicare premiums.

Points to consider regarding a conversion:

How are you going to pay the tax? Again, any time you withdraw funds from a 401(k) or traditional IRA, tax is owed on 100 percent of that money, whether the distribution was a basic withdrawal, an RMD, or a Roth conversion. In addition to the income tax, if the account owner is younger than fifty-nine-and-one-half, it is most likely a 10 percent tax penalty will be assessed. So, if you're under fifty-nine-and-one-half and have a year when your income is lower – reducing your marginal tax rate – you need to weigh the amount of the tax penalty against the decrease in ordinary income tax.

As a tricky sidenote, if you are under fifty-nine-and-one-half and you have tax withheld from your conversion and sent directly to the government, you will not escape the 10 percent penalty.

Did you compare your current tax rate to your estimated future rate? As mentioned above, a good time to consider a Roth is in a year when your taxable income — and thus your marginal tax rate — is lower than normal or lower than expected in the future. A popular conversion strategy is to transfer funds during a period referred to as "the trough years." That is the period after you've retired but before you begin receiving Social Security or are required to begin RMDs. It is easier to manage the tax on the conversion during these years as you have more control over the sources and the amounts of your income.

What is your Roth withdrawal strategy? There are four considerations here.

- Can you leave converted money in the Roth for at least five years? You must leave your converted money in the Roth for at least five years for the withdrawals to be tax-free. That five-year countdown begins on January 1 of the year you made the conversion, even if your conversion date was December 31. This five-year countdown applies in each year you make a conversion.
- Even if you hold the Roth funds for five years, you will still face penalties for withdrawals if you're under fifty-nine-and-one-half.[26]
- The longer you leave funds inside the Roth after the conversion, the more time it can grow and potentially recoup the tax levied on your traditional account's withdrawals. Remember, this money is now growing tax-free. A long growth period may be able to outweigh a loss in your balance due to income tax withholdings at conversion time. Also, an error in estimates of future tax rate margins (i.e., your future rates turned out to be less than the conversion year) can be made up by holding funds in your Roth for many years.[27]
- Planning to use your Roth as a legacy planning tool? There are various rules and options depending on the

---

[26] Kailey Hagen. The Motley Fool. November 16, 2022. "4 Things to Know If You're Considering a Roth IRA Conversion This Year" https://www.fool.com/retirement/2022/11/16/4-things-to-know-if-youre-considering-a-roth-ira-c/

[27] Tim Steffen. Baird Private Wealth Management. October 16, 2023. "The Three Tests Before a Roth Conversion" https://www.bairdwealth.com/insights/wealth-management-perspectives/2023/09/the-three-tests-before-a-roth-conversion/

type of heir, but in most cases the Roth is given additional time to grow tax-free.

Does that make your head spin? Understandable. That's why it's so important to work with a financial professional and tax planner who can help you execute these sorts of tax-efficient strategies and help you understand what you are doing and why.

If you do not have a tax strategy, it is like going on a trip without a map. A road will get you there eventually, but you are going to spend a lot of time in places that you do not want to be, and you are going to spend more money getting there than you need to.

We have strategic relationships with many CPAs, and depending on the project — such as complex estate planning, simple estate planning, charitable planning — we'll use one firm or another depending on your unique needs and goals.

It allows us to utilize tax professionals who know how we think, and we know how they think, so that behind the scenes, we can prepare a plan for the client. Typically at that point, the plan is about 90 percent right. Then we meet with the professional and the client and help the client ask the right questions, because most of the time, clients don't know what to ask.

We can integrate the professionals and coordinate the meetings so that they actually take place. Then, we build an integrated, well-crafted, well-thought-out retirement plan utilizing multiple specialties since, typically, no one person has all the answers.

CHAPTER 3

Market Volatility

U p and down. Roller coaster. Merry-go-round. Bulls and
bears. Peak-to-trough.
Sound familiar? This is the language we use to talk
about the stock market. With volatility and spikes, even our
language is jarring, bracing, and vivid.

Still, financial strategies tend to revolve around market-
based products, and for good reasons. For one thing, there is no
other financial class that packs the same potential for growth,
pound for pound, as stock-based products. Because of growth
potential, inflation challenges, and new opportunities, it may
be unwise to avoid the market entirely.

However, along with the potential for growth is the potential
for loss. At the time this book was written, many of the people
I've seen in my office came in feeling uneasy because of the
economic fallout of the COVID-19 outbreak of 2020, followed
by the economic downturn and the inflation spike that
happened in 2022.

So, how do we balance these factors? How do we try to satisfy
both the need for protection and the need for growth?

For one thing, it is important to recognize the value of
diversity. Now, I'm not just talking about the diversity of assets
among different kinds of stocks, or even different kinds of
stocks and bonds. That's only one kind of diversity. Stocks and
bonds, though different, are both still important market-based
products. Even within a diverse portfolio, most market-based

products tend to rise or fall as a whole, just like an incoming tide. Therefore, a portfolio diverse in only market-sourced products won't automatically preserve your assets during times when the market declines.

In addition to the sort of "horizontal diversity" you have by purchasing a variety of stocks and bonds from different companies, I also suggest you think about "vertical diversity," or diversity among asset classes. This means having different product types, including securities products, bank products, and insurance products — with varying levels of growth potential, liquidity, and protection — all in accordance with your unique situation, goals, and needs.

We take about ten to fifteen minutes at the end of our first appointment and ask a series of questions to help determine the amount of risk each spouse is willing to take with their investments. These questions help produce a unique risk number for each individual.

This risk number can be used to create or modify an existing portfolio so the potential investment portfolio, risk, and the couple's unique risk numbers are in balance.

Even for couples who have been married for decades, this is often an eye-opening experience when each person learns of his or her spouse's openness, or lack of it, to risk.

The Color of Money

When you're looking at the overall diversity of your portfolio, part of the equation is knowing which products fit in what category: what has liquidity, what has asset preservation, and what has growth potential.

Before we dive in, keep in mind these aren't absolutes. You might think of liquidity, growth, and asset preservation as primary colors. While some products will look pretty much yellow, red, or blue, others will have a mix of characteristics, making them more green, orange, or purple.

Growth

I like to think of the growth category as red. It's powerful, it's somewhat volatile, and it's also the category where we have the greatest opportunities for growth and loss. Often, products in the growth category will have a good deal of liquidity but very little protection. These are our market-based products and strategies, and we think of them mostly in shades of red and orange to designate their growth and liquidity. This is usually a good place to be when you're young — think fast cars and flashy leather jackets — but its allure often wanes as you move closer to retirement. Examples of "red" products include:

- Stocks
- Equities
- Exchange-traded funds
- Mutual funds
- Corporate bonds
- Real estate investment trusts
- Speculations
- Alternative investments

Liquidity

Yellow is my liquid category color. I typically recommend having at least enough yellow money to cover six months' to a year's worth of expenses in case of emergency. Yellow assets don't need a lot of growth potential; they just need to be readily available when we need them. The "yellow" category includes assets like:

- Cash
- Money market accounts

Asset Preservation

The color of asset preservation, to me, is blue, which can incorporate products such as annuities. Tranquil, sure — even if it lacks a certain amount of flash. This is the direction I like to see people generally move toward as they're nearing retirement. The red, flashy look of stock market returns and the risk of possible overnight losses are less attractive as we near retirement and look for more consistency and reliability. While this category doesn't come with a lot of liquidity, the products here are backed by an insurance company, a bank, or a government entity. "Blue" products include things such as:

- Certificates of deposit (backed by banks)
- Government-based bonds (backed by the U.S. government)
- Life insurance (backed by insurance companies)
- Annuities (backed by insurance companies)

Market-based products can be used in almost every portfolio but in such a way that they are combined with a diversified portfolio of stocks, bonds, and mutual funds, among other types of investments.

Everything needs to work together to achieve the goals and objectives of an individual's unique circumstances, and your investments are part of the overall strategy.

An investor should complement his or her unique risk numbers with accounts that have little or no risk. These accounts can be used for income when the market-based accounts are in decline.

401(k)s

I want to take a second to specifically address a product many retirees will be using to build their retirement income: the 401(k) and other retirement accounts. Any of these retirement accounts (IRAs, 401(k)s, 403(b)s, etc.) are basically "tax wrappers." What do I mean by that? Well, depending on your plan provider, a 401(k) could include target-date funds, passively managed products, stocks, bonds, mutual funds, or even variable, fixed, and fixed index annuities, all collected in one place and governed by rules (a.k.a. the "tax wrapper"). These rules govern how much money you can put inside, what ways you can put it in, when you will pay taxes on it, and when you can take the money out. Inside the 401(k), each of the products inside the "tax wrapper" might have its own fees or commissions in addition to the management fee you pay on the 401(k) itself.

Now, fees can be troublesome. You can't get something for nothing, and fees are how many financial companies and professionals make a living. Yet, it's important to recognize even a fee with a fraction of a percentage point is money out of your pocket — money that represents not just the one-time fee of today but also an opportunity cost. For example, consider how a $100,000 IRA that earns 6 percent over a twenty-five-year period without investment fees would earn $430,000. But if just a 0.5 percent fee was factored into that investment, the IRA would be worth $379,000 in twenty-five years — a $50,500 decrease. For someone close to retirement, how much do you think fees may have cost over their lifetime?

Even for those close to retirement, it's important to look at management fees and assess if you think you're getting what you pay for. Over the course of ten years, those costs can add up, and you may have decades ahead of you in which you will need to rely on your assets.

Dollar-Cost Averaging

With 401(k)s and other market-based retirement products, dollar-cost averaging is a concept that can work in your favor when you are investing for the long term. When the market is trending up, if you are consistently paying in money, month over month, great; your investments can grow, and you are adding to your assets. When the market takes a dip, no problem; your dollars buy more shares at a lower price. At some point, we hope the market will rebound, in which case your shares can grow and possibly be more valuable than they were before. This concept is what we call "dollar-cost averaging."

While it can't ensure a profit or guarantee against losses, it's a time-tested strategy for investing in a volatile market.

However, when you are in retirement, this strategy may work against you. You may have heard of "reverse" dollar-cost averaging. Before, when the market lost ground, you were "bargain-shopping"; your dollars purchased more assets at a reduced price. When you are in retirement, you are no longer the purchaser; you are selling. So, in a down market, you have to sell more assets to make the same amount of money as what you made in a favorable market.

I've had lots of people step into my office to talk to me about this, emphasizing how their advisor says, "The market always bounces back, and I have to just hold on for the long term."

There's some basis for this thinking; thus far, the market has always rebounded to higher heights than before. But this is no guarantee, and the prospect of potentially higher returns in five years may not be very helpful in retirement if you are relying on the income from those returns to pay this month's electric bill, for example.

Market-based products can be used in almost every portfolio but in such a way that they are combined with a diversified portfolio of stocks, bonds, and mutual funds, among other types of investments.

Everything needs to work together to achieve the goals and objectives of an individual's unique circumstances, and your investments are part of the overall strategy.

An investor should complement his or her unique risk numbers with accounts that have little or no risk and can be used for income when the market-based accounts are negative.[*]

Is There a "Perfect" Product?

To bring us back around to the discussion of asset preservation, growth, and liquidity, the ideal product would be a "ten" in all

---

[*] Diversification does not guarantee against loss; it is a method used to help manage risk.

three categories, right? Completely guaranteed, doubling in size every few years, and accessible whenever you want. Does such a product exist? Absolutely not.

Instead of running in circles looking for that perfect product, the silver bullet, the unicorn of financial strategies, it's more important to circle back to the concept of a balanced, asset-diverse portfolio.

This is why it could be prudent to work with a knowledgeable financial professional who knows what various financial products can do and how to use them in your personal retirement strategy.[*]

---

[*] Investing involves risk, including the potential loss of principal. No investment strategy can guarantee a profit or protect against loss in periods of declining values. Any references to protection benefits or guaranteed/lifetime income streams refer only to fixed insurance products, not securities or investment products. Insurance and annuity product guarantees are backed by the financial strength and claims-paying ability of the issuing insurance company.

Retirement Income

R etirement. For many of us, it's what we've saved for and dreamed of, pinning our hopes to a magical someday. Is that someday full of traveling? Is it filled with grandkids? Gardening? Maybe your fondest dream is simply never having to work again, never having to clock in or be accountable to someone else.

Your ability to do these things all hinges on *income*. Without the money to support these dreams, even a basic level of work-free lifestyle is unsustainable. That's why planning for your income in retirement is so foundational. But where do we begin?

It's easy to feel overwhelmed by this question. Some may feel the urge to amass a large lump sum and then try to put it all in one product — insurance, investments, liquid assets — to provide all the growth, liquidity, and income they need. Instead, I think you need a more balanced approach. After all, retirement planning isn't magic. As I mention elsewhere, there is no single product that can be all things to all people (or even all things to one person). No approach works unilaterally for everyone. That's why it's important to talk to a financial professional who can help you lay down the basics and take you step-by-step through the process. Not only will you have the assurance you have addressed the areas you need to, but you will also have an ally who can help you break down the process and help keep you from feeling overwhelmed.

Sources of Income

Thinking of all the pieces of your retirement expenses might be intimidating. But, like cleaning out a junk drawer or revisiting that garage remodel, once you have laid everything out, you can begin to sort things into categories.

Once you have a good overall picture of where your expenses will lie, you can start stacking up the resources to cover them.

Social Security

Social Security is a guaranteed, inflation-adjusted federal insurance program that plays a significant part in most of our retirement plans. From delaying until you've reached full retirement age or beyond to examining spousal benefits, as I discuss elsewhere in this book, there is plenty you can do to try to make the most of this monthly benefit. As with all your retirement income sources, it's important to consider ways to make this resource stretch to provide the most bang for your situation.

Pension

Another generally reliable source of retirement income for you might be a pension, if you are one of the lucky people who still has one.

If you don't have a pension, go ahead and skim on to the next section. If you do have a pension, keep on reading.

Because your pension can be such a central piece of your retirement income plan, you will want to put some thought into answering basic questions about it.

How well is your pension funded? Since the heyday of the pension plan, companies and governments have neglected to fund their pension obligations, causing a persistent problem with this otherwise reliable asset.

Consider the factors at play, though. Pensions had been underfunded and gained a boost from strong market performance, most recently in 2021.[28] What happens to the solvency of those pension funds if the market declines?

It can be worthwhile to keep tabs on your pension's health and know what your options are for withdrawing from it. Typically, you have one chance at electing the distribution option at your retirement with no recourse to change at a later date, so you will want to look at all options before making a final decision. If you have already retired and made those decisions, this may be a foregone conclusion. If not, it pays to know what you can expect and what decisions you can make, such as taking spousal options to cover your spouse if they outlive you.

Also, some companies are incentivizing lump-sum payouts of pensions to reduce the companies' payment liabilities. If that's the case with your employer, talk to your financial professional to see if it might be prudent to do something like that or if it might be better to stick with lifetime payments or other options.

Let's look at someone who has a choice on his pension. He could take it in a lump sum and transfer it as an IRA rollover, which would allow him to continue to defer the tax until he was ready to withdraw the money.

As an alternative, he could take his full pension for his lifetime or for a reduced amount that would pay up to 100 percent to his wife if he died first.

Through a pension-maximization analysis, we could help him determine if it makes sense to take his pension in installments with reduced benefits. That way, at his death, his spouse would continue receiving the same amount.

This absolutely must be done on a case-by-case basis.

---

[28] The Pew Charitable Trusts. November 8, 2023. "Public Retirement Systems Need Sustainable Policies to Navigate Volatile Financial Markets" https://www.pewtrusts.org/en/research-and-analysis/issue-briefs/2023/11/public-retirement-systems-need-sustainable-policies-to-navigate-volatile-financial-markets

The other advantage is it creates guaranteed income. Depending on the funding of the pension, that guarantee could be diminished or subjected to more risk in the future.

Because pension funding is a direct liability to corporations regardless of their profits, most don't offer pensions anymore. They offer 401(k) accounts instead.

Then, each year, companies can determine if they will contribute employer funds to the accounts.

That leaves the employee with the burden of creating additional income at retirement.

Your 401(k) and IRA

One "modern way" to save for retirement is in a 401(k) or IRA (or their nonprofit or governmental equivalents). These tax-advantaged accounts are, in my opinion, a poor substitute for pensions, but one of the biggest disservices we do to ourselves is not taking full advantage of them in the first place. While the average 401(k) balance for Americans between the ages of forty and forty-nine is $105,500, the median account balance is much lower. The median, which separates half of accounts with higher balances and half with lower balances, is just $34,100.[29]

Also, if you have changed jobs over the years, do the work of tracking down any benefits from your past employers. You might have an IRA here or a 401(k) there; keep track of those so you can pull them together and look at those assets when you're ready to look at establishing sources of retirement income.

Do You Have ...

- Life insurance?
- Annuities?

---

[29] Cheyenne DeVon. CNBC. July 13, 2023. "Here's how much Americans in their 40s have in their 401(k)s"
https://www.cnbc.com/2023/07/13/fidelity-how-much-americans-in-their-40s-have-in-their-401ks.html

- Long-term care insurance?
- Any passive income sources?
- Stock and bond portfolios?
- Liquid assets? (What's in your bank account?)
- Alternative investments?
- Rental properties?

If you are going through the work of sitting with a financial professional, it's important to look at your full retirement income picture and pull together *all* your assets, no matter how big or small. From the free insurance policy offered at your bank to the sizable investment in your brother-in-law's modestly successful furniture store, you want to know where your money is.

It can be hard to keep track of all your accounts.

A friend told me of one woman and her husband who were doing all right early in their retirement but wondered when they would need to start dipping into their 401(k) savings.

Then, in a casual conversation, the wife learned through a former co-worker that her company had a pension plan that she knew nothing about. She assumed there was not much in it, but she contacted the company and learned she was entitled to $1,000 a month for the rest of her life.

It was an amazing find that, when added to their other monthly income, made a dramatic difference in when they would need to start dipping into their retirement savings.

It pays, often literally, to do the work of collecting information on all your potential accounts.

Retirement Income Needs

How much income will you need in retirement? How do you determine that? A lot of people work toward a random number, thinking, "If I can just have a million dollars, I'll be comfortable in retirement!" Don't get me wrong; it is possible to save up a lot of money and then retire in the hopes you can keep your monthly expenses lower than some set estimation. But I think this carries a general risk of running out of money. Instead, I work with my clients to find out what their current and projected income needs are and then work from there to see how we might cover any gaps between what they have and what they want.

Goals and Dreams

I like to start with your pie in the sky. Do you find yourself planning for your vacations more thoroughly than you do your retirement? Maybe it's because planning a vacation is less stressful: Having a week at the beach go awry is, well, a walk on the beach compared to running out of money in retirement. Whatever the case, perhaps it would be better if you thought of your retirement as a vacation in and of itself — no clocking in, no boss, no overtime. If you felt unlimited by financial strain, what would you do?

Would an endless vacation for you mean Paris and Rome? Would it mean mentoring at children's clubs or serving at the local soup kitchen? Or maybe it would mean deepening your ties to those immediately around you — neighbors, friends, and family. Maybe it would mean more time to take part in the hobbies and activities you love. Have you been considering a second (or even third) act as a small-business owner, turning a hobby or passion into a revenue source?

This is your time to daydream and answer the question: If you could do anything, what would you do?

After that, it's a matter of putting a dollar amount on it. What are the costs of round-the-world travel? One couple I know said their highest priority in retirement was being able to take each of their grandchildren on a cross-country vacation every year. That's a pretty specific goal — one that is reasonably easy to nail down a budget for.

Most individuals, at least when encouraged, have dreams for retirement.

Before we help people retire, we always want to find out what they are going to do in their retirement with all this extra time.

At the end of your Living the Dream consultation, we often give individuals a gift certificate of $10 or $15 each to a restaurant near our office to enjoy a slice of pie and some coffee and dream about their retirement.

Retirement should be about the things you always wanted to do but could not because you were too busy working.

It is also a fun time to then consider, with the help of an advisor, how much money those dreams will cost. Then, through planning, those dreams can become a reality.

Current Budget

Compiling a current expense report is one of the trickiest pieces of retirement preparation. Many people assume the expenses of their lives in retirement will be lower. After all, there will be no drive to work, no need for a formal wardrobe, and — perhaps most impactful of all — no more saving for retirement!

Yet, we often underestimate our daily spending habits. That's why I typically ask my clients to bring in their bank statements for the past year — they are reflective of your *actual* spending, not just what you think you're spending.

Some people come in with a detailed budget, which, of course, is helpful for discussion. Obviously, the more detailed, the better, but if not, we can always start with at least the amount of money someone is bringing home as a paycheck after taxes, health insurance, and benefits, such as 401(k) plans, because that's what the individual is living on now. We can add in taxes as we develop the retirement plan.

It's important to understand that a lot of items on an individual's budget before he retires may or may not exist or may be different when an individual retires.

For example, the individual probably will not contribute to a 401(k) after retirement.

I can't count the number of times I have sat with a couple, asked them about their spending, and heard them throw out a number that seemed incredibly low. When I ask them where the number came from, they usually say they estimated based on their total bills. Yet, our spending is so much more than our mortgage, utilities, cable, phone, car, grocery, or credit card bills.

"What about clothes?" I ask, "Or dining out? What about gifts and coffees and last-minute birthday cards?" That's when the lights come on.

This is why I suggest collecting a year's worth of information. There is usually no such thing as a one-time purchase. Did you buy new furniture? Even if that is a rarity, do you think that will be the last time you *ever* buy furniture?

Many people are surprised when presented with a true picture of their income needs at retirement. Better to be surprised now before retirement than after retirement, right?

Let's look at a husband and wife who, say, are absolutely adamant they can live on $7,000 a month after taxes.

As part of our Sustainable Retirement process, we then identify that they have in fact been living on $10,500 a month since they retired. They are not considering all their different sources of income because a lot of funds are directly deposited into their accounts.

We can then do an audit of their checking and savings accounts for income and withdrawals, and we'll be proven correct.

With that proof, we can help them understand we are working with them, not against them, and can construct a Sustainable Retirement Plan that gives them confidence going forward that the higher amount of monthly income is still achievable.

Another hefty expense is spending on the kids. Many of the couples I work with are quick to help their adult children, whether it's something like letting them live in the basement, paying for college, babysitting, paying an occasional bill, or contributing to a grandchild's college fund. Research concluded that 54 percent of those in the Gen Z and millennial age groups lean on parents for financial support. Among those, 23 percent are heavily supported by parents.[30]

My clients sometimes protest that what they do for their grown children can stop in retirement. They don't *need* to help. But I get it. Parents like to feel needed. And, while you never want to neglect saving for retirement in favor of taking on financial risks (like your child's student debt), the parents who help their adult children do so in part because it helps them feel fulfilled.

When it comes down to expenses, including (and especially) spending on your family, don't make your initial calculations based on what you *could* whittle your budget down to if you *had* to. Instead, start from where you are. Who wants to live off a bare-bones bank account in retirement?

Other Expenses

Once you have nailed down your current budget and your dreams or goals for retirement, there are a few other outstanding pieces to think about — some expenses many people don't take the time to consider before making and executing a plan. But I'm assuming you want to get it right, so let's take a look.

Housing

Do you know where you want to live in retirement? This makes up a substantial piece of your income puzzle — since the typical American household owns a home, and it's generally their largest asset.

---

[30] Experian. June 27, 2023. "Most Gen Zers and millennials still rely on parents for financial support and feel ashamed asking for help"
https://www.experianplc.com/newsroom/press-releases/2023/most-gen-zers-and-millennials-still-rely-on-parents-for-financial-support-and-feel-ashamed-asking-for-help

Some people prefer to live right where they are for as long as they can. Others have been waiting for retirement to pull the trigger on an ambitious move, like purchasing a new house, or even downsizing. Whatever your plans and whatever your reasons, there are quite a few things to consider.

Mortgage

Do you still have a mortgage? What may have been a nice tax boon in your working years could turn into a financial burden in your retirement. After all, when you are on a limited income, a mortgage is just one more bill sapping your financial strength. It is something to put some thought into, whether you plan to age in place or are considering moving to your dream home, buying a house out of state, or living in a retirement community.

Upkeep and Taxes

A house without a mortgage still requires annual taxes. While it's tempting to think of this as a once-a-year expense, when you have limited earning potential, your annual tax bill might be something into which you should put a little more forethought.

The costs of homeownership aren't just monetary. When you find yourself dealing with more house than you need, it can drain your time and energy. From keeping clutter at bay to keeping the lawn mower running, upkeep can be extensive and expensive. For some, that's a challenge they heartily accept and can comfortably take on. For others, the idea of yard work or cleaning an area larger than they need feels foolish.

For instance, Peggy discovered after her knee replacement that most of her house was inaccessible to her when she was laid up.

"It felt ridiculous to pay someone else to dust and vacuum a house I was only living in 40 percent of!"

Practicality and Adaptability

Erik and Marla are looking to retire within the next two decades. They just sold their old three-bedroom ranch-style house. Their twins are in high school, and the couple has wanted to "upgrade" for years. Now they live in a gorgeous 1940s three-story house with all the kitchen space they ever wanted, five sprawling bedrooms, and a library and media room for themselves and their children. Within months of moving in, the couple realized a house perfect for their active teens would no longer be perfect for them in five to fifteen years.

"We are paying the mortgage for this house, but we've started saving for the next one," said Marla, "because who wants to climb two flights of stairs to their bedroom when they're seventy-eight?"

Others I know have encountered a similar situation in their personal lives. After a health crisis, one couple found the luxurious tub for two they toiled to install had become a specter of a bad slip and a potential safety risk. It's important to think through what your physical reality could be. I always emphasize to my clients that they should plan for whatever their long-term future might hold, but it's amazing how many people don't give it much thought.

Contracts and Regulations

If you are looking into a cross-country move, be aware of new tax tables or local ordinances in the area where you are looking to move. After all, you don't want to experience sticker-shock when you are looking at downsizing or reducing your bills in retirement.

Along the same lines, if you are moving into a retirement community, be sure to look at the fine print. What happens if you must move into a different situation for long-term care? Will you be penalized? Will you be responsible for replacing your slot in the community? What are all the fees, and what do they cover?

Inflation

As I write this in 2025, America has experienced a wave of inflation following a lengthy period of low inflation. Inflation zoomed to 9.1 percent in June 2022, its highest mark since November 1981.[31] Consequently, inflation dropped to a three-year low of 2.4 percent in September 2024 after reaching a forty-year high in 2022 — quite the roller coaster.[32]

Core inflation is yet another measurement that excludes goods with prices that tend to be more volatile, such as food and energy costs. Core inflation for a twelve-month period ending in October 2024 was 3.3 percent.[33]

However, inflation isn't a one-time bump; it has a cumulative effect. Again, that can impact the price of groceries more than other goods. Even with relatively low inflation over the past few decades, an item you bought in 1997 for $2 will cost about $3.92 today.[34] Want to go to a show? A $20 ticket in 1997 would cost $45.18 in 2024.[35]

What if we hit a stretch in retirement like the late seventies and early eighties, when annual inflation rates of 10 percent became the norm? It may be wise to consider some extra padding in your retirement income plan to account for any potential increase in inflation in the future.

---

[31] Trading Economics. 2024. "United States Inflation Rate" https://tradingeconomics.com/united-states/inflation-cpi

[32] Ibid.

[33] YCharts. US Core Inflation Rate. https://ycharts.com/indicators/us_core_inflation_rate#:~:text=Basic%20Info,long%20term%20average%20of%203.68%25.

[34] in2013dollars.com. 2024. "$2 in 1997 is worth $3.92 today" https://www.in2013dollars.com/us/inflation/1997?amount=2

[35] in2013dollars.com. 2024. "Admission to movies, theaters, and concerts priced at $20 in 1997 ->$45.18 in 2024" https://www.in2013dollars.com/Admission-to-movies,-theaters,-and-concerts/price-inflation

Shrinkflation

Another important yet often overlooked factor to consider is called "shrinkflation." Essentially a form of hidden inflation, shrinkflation signifies a reduction in packaging while retaining a similar price as before.

For example, as you walk down a grocery store aisle, you spot your favorite pickles. The jar still costs the same — roughly $5 — and you add it to your cart. Then you get home, and the container seems different after digging out a few crispy dills. You examine the jar and discover it contains fewer ounces than previous jars you purchased. However, you paid roughly the same price for your pickles.

Now, move over to the aisle featuring salty snacks. You might notice a sale on a certain brand of chips, though you must buy three or four bags to receive a discount promoted by the store. You decide to purchase that many bags to capitalize on the lower price. When you get home, you notice the packaging is smaller than you anticipated. The deal you accepted may not have been as thrifty as you perceived.

Shrinkflation can be a way for companies to quietly boost, or retain, profit margins without having to change much else — essentially, they are simply charging the same price for less product. Companies do this because customers are more likely to spot price increases than size reductions. However, research has also shown that these shrinkflation tactics can backfire into negative consumer perceptions of their brands once they come to light. Who wants to pay the same for less, especially when they have already grown accustomed to getting more for their money's worth?[36]

---

[36] Daniel Liberto. Investopedia. November 16, 2023. "Shrinkflation: What It Is, Reasons for It, How to Spot It" https://www.investopedia.com/terms/s/shrinkflation.asp

Aging

Also, in the expense category, think about longevity. We all hope to age gracefully. However, it's important to face the prospect of aging with a sense of realism.

For many families, the elephant in the room is long-term care. No one wants to admit they will likely need it, but estimates indicate almost 70 percent of us will.[37] Aging is a significant piece of retirement income planning because you'll want to figure out how to set aside money for your care, either at home or away from it. The more comfortable you get with discussing your wishes and plans with your loved ones, the easier planning for the financial side of it can be.

I denote health care and potential long-term care costs in more detail elsewhere in this book, but suffice it to say nursing home care tends to be very expensive and typically isn't something you get to choose when you will need.

It isn't just the costs of long-term care that pose a concern in living longer. It's also about covering the possible costs of everything else associated with living longer. For instance, if Henry retires from his job as a biochemical engineer at age sixty-five, perhaps he plans to have a very decent income for twenty years until he turns eighty-five. But what if he lives until he's ninety-five? That's a whole third — ten years — more of personal income he will need.

Putting It All Together

Whew! So, you have pulled together what you have, and you have a pretty good idea of where you want to be. Now, you and your financial professional can go about the work of arranging what assets you *have* to cover what you *need* — and how you might try to cover any gaps.

---

[37] Moll Law Group. 2024. "The Cost of Long-Term Care"
https://www.molllawgroup.com/the-cost-of-long-term-care.html

Like the proverbial man in the Bible who built his house on a rock, I like to help my clients figure out how to cover their day-to-day living expenses — their needs — with insurance and other guaranteed income sources like pensions and Social Security.

We use our Sustainable Retirement Plan process to help determine if a couple can retire. This helps us identify problem areas that they should correct as soon as possible and helps us give them solutions so that they can have more confidence in their retirement.

Again, you should keep in mind there isn't one single financial vehicle, asset, or source to fill all your needs, and that's okay. One of the challenges of planning for your income in retirement concerns figuring out what products and strategies to use. You can release some of that stress when you accept the fact you will probably need a diverse portfolio — potentially with bonds, stocks, insurance, and other income sources — not just one massive money pile.

One way to help shore up your income gaps is by working with your financial professional and a qualified tax advisor to help mitigate your tax exposure. If you have a 401(k) or IRA, a tax advisor in your corner may be able to help you figure out how and when to take distributions from your account in a way that doesn't push you into a higher tax bracket. Or you might learn of ways to use tax-advantaged bonds more effectively. Effective tax planning isn't necessarily about "adding" to your income. Especially regarding retirement, it's less about what you make than it is about what you keep. Paying a lower tax bill keeps more money in your pocket, which is where you want it when it comes to retirement income.

Now you can look at ways to cover your remaining retirement goals. Are there products like long-term care insurance specific to a certain kind of expense you anticipate? Is there a particular asset you want to use for your "play" money — money for trips and gifts for the grandkids? Is there any way you can portion off money for those charitable legacy plans?

Once you have analyzed your income wants, needs, and the assets necessary to realistically cover them, you may have a gap. The masterstroke of a competent financial professional will be to help you figure out how you will cover that gap. Will you need to cut out a round of golf a week? Maybe skip the new car? Or will you need to take more substantial action?

One way to cover an income gap is to consider working longer or even part-time before retirement and even after that magical calendar date. This may not be the best "plan" for you; disabilities, work demands, and physical or emotional limitations can hinder the best-laid plans to continue working. However, if it is physically possible for you, this is one considerable way to help your assets last for more than one reason.

In fact, 55 percent of the Americans responding to a survey report they plan to work part-time after retiring, while 15 percent expect compensation from work to be their primary source of retirement income.[38]

We all probably can imagine someone's frustration at having to work five or six years before being able to retire.

With our knowledge and expertise to build an individualized Sustainable Retirement Plan, though, we might be able to present someone with good news earlier than expected.

Sometimes, it takes more than one meeting to convince people that their money will last their lifetimes.

Imagine a client getting upset with me when I ask if she enjoyed working that day. She might be irked because she's already said she no longer wants to work.

But imagine her frustration turning to relief and even elation when I present what all her assets combined mean for retirement. She can quit today with confidence that her money will last her lifetime.

We can help dreams like this come true.

------

[38] Kerry Hannon. Yahoo! Finance. July 15, 2023. "Future retirees plan to work longer, partly due to savings shortfalls"
https://finance.yahoo.com/news/future-retirees-plan-to-work-longer-partly-due-to-savings-shortfalls-160038419.html

Remember, when you're retired, you no longer have an employer paying you a steady check. It's up to you to make sure you have saved and planned for the income you need.

CHAPTER 5

Social Security

Social Security is often the foundation of retirement income. Backed by the strength of the U.S. Treasury, it provides perhaps the most dependable paycheck you will have in retirement.

From the time you collect your first paycheck from the job that made you a bona fide taxpayer (for me, it was at Wesselman's Supermarket in the Lawndale Shopping Center in Evansville), you are paying into the grand old Social Security system.

What grew and developed out of the pressures of the Great Depression has become one of the most popular government programs in the country, and if you pay in for the equivalent of ten years or more, you, too, can benefit from the Social Security program.

Now, before we get into the nitty-gritty of Social Security, I'd like to address a current concern: Will Social Security still be there for you when you reach retirement age?

The Future of Social Security

This question is ever-present as headlines trumpet an underfunded Social Security program, alongside the sea of baby boomers retiring in droves and the comparatively smaller pool of younger people who are funding the system.

The Social Security Administration itself acknowledges this concern as each Social Security statement now contains a link to its website (ssa.gov) and a page entitled, "Will Social Security Be There For Me?"

The Social Security Fairness Act, a legislative measure enacted in early 2025, repealed the Windfall Elimination Provision (WEP) and Government Pension Offset (GPO), which have historically reduced Social Security benefits for retirees with pensions from jobs not covered by Social Security.

The new legislation helps to ensure fairer benefits for those who worked in both public and private sectors, improving income predictability and financial planning for future retirees. Removing the previous provisions simplifies benefit calculations, eliminates past penalties, and provides retirees with a steadier, more reliable income.[39] Staying informed about Social Security updates is essential. Updates directly impact retirement decisions.

Just a reminder, as if you needed one, that nothing in life is guaranteed. For example, as a result of the 2025 tax bill (the "OBBB"), the Social Security trust fund is expected to be depleted by 2032, prompting the Social Security Board of Trustees to estimate that only 76 percent of scheduled benefits can be paid.[40]

Before you get too discouraged, though, here are a few thoughts to keep you going:

- Even if the program is only paying 75 to 78 cents on the dollar for scheduled benefits, this is notably not zero.
- The Social Security Administration has made changes in the distant and near past to help protect the fund's

[39] Trina Paul. Investopedia. January 6, 2025. "Biden Signs Social Security Law That Boosts Benefits For Public Sector Retirees" https://www.investopedia.com/bill-that-boosts-social-security-benefits-for-retired-federal-workers-goes-into-law-8768459

[40] Committee for a Responsible Federal Budget. June 27, 2025. "OBBBA Would Accelerate Social Security & Medicare Insolvency" https://www.crfb.org/blogs/obbba-would-accelerate-social-security-medicare-insolvent

solvency, including increasing retirement ages and striking certain filing strategies.

- There are many changes Congress could make, and lawmakers routinely discuss ideas for amending the system, such as further increasing full retirement age and eligibility.
- One thing no one is seriously discussing? Reneging on current obligations to retirees or the soon-to-retire.

Take heart. The real answer to the question, "Will Social Security be there for me?" is still yes.

This question is important to consider when you look at how much we, as a nation, rely on this program. Did you know Social Security benefits replace about 37 percent of a person's original income when they retire?[41]

If you ask me, that's a pretty significant piece of your retirement income puzzle.

Another caveat? You may not realize this, but no one can legally "advise" you about your Social Security benefits.

"But, Brad, you may be thinking, "isn't that part of what you do? And what about that nice gentleman at the Social Security Administration office I spoke with on the phone?"

Don't get me wrong. Social Security Administration employees know their stuff. They are trained to understand policies and programs, and they are usually pretty quick to tell you what you can and cannot do. But the government specifically stipulates that because Social Security is a benefit you alone have paid into and earned, your Social Security decisions are *also* yours alone.

When it comes to financial professionals, we can't push you in any direction, but — there's a big but here — working with a well-informed financial professional is still incredibly handy for your Social Security decisions. Why? Because someone who's

---

[41] Center on Budget and Policy Priorities. April 17, 2023. "Top Ten Facts About Social Security"
https://www.cbpp.org/sites/default/files/atoms/files/8-8-16socsec.pdf

worth their salt will know what withdrawal strategies might pertain to your specific situation and will ask questions that can help you determine what you are looking for when it comes to your Social Security.

For instance, some people want the highest possible monthly benefit. Others want to start their benefits early, and not always because of financial need. I heard about one man who called in to start his Social Security payments the day he qualified just because he liked to think of it as the government paying back a debt it owed him, and he enjoyed the feeling of receiving a check from Uncle Sam.

Whatever your reasons, questions, or feelings regarding Social Security, the decision is yours alone, but working with a financial professional can help you put your options in perspective by showing you — both with industry knowledge and with proprietary software or planning processes — where your benefits fit into your overall strategy for retirement income.

Full Retirement Age

When it comes to Social Security, it seems like many people only think so far as "yes." They don't take the time to understand the various options available. Instead, because it is common knowledge you can begin your benefits at age sixty-two, that's what many of us do. While more people are opting to delay benefits, age sixty-two is still a popular age to start.[42]

Some people fail to understand that starting benefits early may leave significant money on the table. You see, the Social Security Administration bases your monthly benefit on two factors: your earnings history and your full retirement age (FRA).

---

[42] Emily Brandon and Erica Sandberg. U.S. News & World Report. August 14, 2023. "The Most Popular Ages to Collect Social Security" https://money.usnews.com/money/retirement/social-security/articles/the-most-popular-ages-to-collect-social-security

From your earnings history, the SSA pulls the thirty-five years you made the most money and uses a mathematical indexing formula to figure out a monthly average from those years. If you paid into the system for less than thirty-five years, then every year you didn't pay in will be counted as a zero.

Once they have calculated what your monthly earnings would be at FRA, the government then calculates what to put on your check based on how close you are to FRA. FRA was originally set at sixty-five, but as the population aged and lifespans lengthened, the government shifted FRA later and later, based on an individual's year of birth. Check out the following chart to see when you will reach FRA.[43] The maximum benefit for a worker retiring at full retirement age is $4,018 in 2025.[44]

---

[43] Social Security Administration. 2024. "Starting Your Retirement Benefits Early"
https://www.ssa.gov/benefits/retirement/planner/agereduction.html
[44] Rachel Christian. Bankrate. October 24, 2024. "Social Security benefits in 2025: 5 big changes retirees should plan for"
https://www.bankrate.com/retirement/social-security-benefits-changes-in-2025/.

Age to Receive Full Social Security Benefits*	
(Called "full retirement age" [FRA] or "normal retirement age.")	
Year of Birth*	FRA
1937 or earlier	65
1938	65 and 2 months
1939	65 and 4 months
1940	65 and 6 months
1941	65 and 8 months
1942	65 and 10 months
1943-1954	66
1955	66 and 2 months
1956	66 and 4 months
1957	66 and 6 months
1958	66 and 8 months
1959	66 and 10 months
1960 and later	67
*If you were born on January 1 of any year, you should refer to the previous year. (If you were born on the 1st of the month, we figure your benefit [and your full retirement age] as if your birthday was in the previous month.)[45]	

When you reach FRA, you are eligible to receive 100 percent of whatever the Social Security Administration calculates as your full monthly benefit.

Starting at age sixty-two, for every year before FRA you claim benefits, your monthly check is reduced by 5 percent or more.

---

[45] Social Security Administration. 2024. "Normal Retirement Age" https://www.ssa.gov/oact/progdata/nra.html

Conversely, for every year you delay taking benefits past FRA, your monthly benefit increases by 8 percent (until age seventy — after that, there is no monetary advantage to delaying Social Security benefits). While your circumstances and needs may vary, a lot of financial professionals still urge people to at least consider delaying until they reach age seventy.

Why wait?[46]

Taking benefits early could affect your monthly check by _____.								
62	63	64	65	66	FRA 67	68	69	70
-30%	-25%	-20%	-13.3%	-6.7%	0	+8%	+16%	+24%

[47]

My Social Security

If you are over thirty, you have probably received a notice from the Social Security Administration telling you to activate something called "My Social Security." This is a handy way to learn more about your particular benefit options, keep track of your earnings record, and calculate the benefits you have accrued over the years.

Essentially, My Social Security is an online account you can activate to see your personal Social Security picture. You can access this information at www.ssa.gov/myaccount. This can be extremely helpful when it comes to planning for income in retirement and figuring out the difference between your anticipated income versus anticipated expenses.

---

[46] Social Security Administration. 2024. "Retirement Benefits" https://www.ssa.gov/pubs/EN-05-10035.pdf
[47] Social Security Administration. 2024. "Effect of Early or Delayed Retirement on Retirement Benefits" https://www.ssa.gov/oact/ProgData/ar_drc.html

COLA

Social Security is a largely guaranteed piece of the retirement puzzle: If you get a statement that reads you should expect $1,000 a month, you can be sure you will receive $1,000 a month. But there is one variable detail, and that is something called the cost-of-living adjustment (COLA).

The COLA is an increase in your monthly check meant to address inflation in everyday life. After all, your expenses will likely continue to experience inflation in retirement, but you will no longer have the opportunity for raises, bonuses, or promotions you had when you were working. Instead, Social Security receives an annual cost-of-living increase tied to the Department of Labor's Consumer Price Index for Urban Wage Earners and Clerical Workers (CPI-W). If the CPI-W measurement shows inflation rose a certain amount for regular goods and services, then Social Security recipients will see that reflected in their COLA.

COLA adjustments have climbed as high as 14.3 percent (1980), and in 2023, they reached 8.7 percent — the largest increase in more than forty years. In a no- or low-inflation environment (such as in 2010, 2011, and 2016), Social Security recipients will not receive an adjustment.[48] The 2025 adjustment decreased to 2.5 percent from 3.2 percent in 2024.[49]

Some view the COLA as a perk, bump, or bonus, but in reality, it works more like this: Your mom sends you to the store with $2.50 for a gallon of milk. Milk costs exactly $2.50. The next week, you go back with that same amount, but it is now $2.52 for a gallon, so you go back to Mom, and she gives you 2 cents. You aren't bringing home more milk — it just costs more money.

---

[48] Social Security Administration. 2024. "Cost-Of-Living Adjustments" https://www.ssa.gov/oact/cola/colaseries.html
[49] Social Security Administration. 2024. "Cost-of-Living Adjustment (COLA) Information for 2024" https://www.ssa.gov/cola/

The COLA is less about "making more money" and more about keeping seniors' purchasing power from eroding when inflation is a big factor. Still, don't let that detract from your enthusiasm about COLAs. After all, what if Mom's solution was: "Here's the same $2.50. Try to find pennies from somewhere else to get that milk!"?

Spousal Benefits

We've talked about FRA, but another big Social Security decision involves spousal benefits.

If you or your spouse has a long stretch of zeros in your earnings history — perhaps if one of you stayed home for years, caring for children or sick relatives — you may want to consider filing for spousal benefits instead of filing on your own earnings history. A spousal benefit can be up to 50 percent of the primary wage earner's benefit at full retirement age.

To begin drawing a spousal benefit, you must be at least sixty-two years old, and the primary wage earner must have already filed for their benefit. While there are penalties for taking spousal benefits early, you cannot earn credits for delaying past full retirement age.[50]

As I wrote, the spousal benefit can be a big deal for those who don't have a very long pay history, but it's important to weigh your own earned benefits against the option of withdrawing based on a fraction of your spouse's benefits.

To look at how this could play out, let's use a hypothetical couple: Mary Jane, who is sixty, and Peter, who is sixty-two.

Let's say Peter's benefit at FRA — in his case, sixty-seven — would be $1,600. If Peter begins his benefits right now (five years before FRA), his monthly check will be $1,120. If Mary Jane begins taking spousal benefits in two years at the earliest date possible, her monthly benefits will be reduced to $560 per month.

---

[50] Social Security Administration. 2024. "Benefits For Your Family" https://www.ssa.gov/benefits/retirement/planner/applying7.html

What if Peter and Mary Jane both wait until FRA? At sixty-seven, Peter begins taking his full benefit of $1,600 a month. Two years later, when she reaches age sixty-seven, Mary Jane will qualify for $800 a month (half of Peter's FRA benefit). By waiting until FRA, the couple's monthly benefit goes from $1,680 to $2,400.

What if Peter delays until age seventy to get his maximum possible benefit? For each year past FRA he delays, his monthly benefits increase by 8 percent. This means that at seventy, he could file for a monthly benefit of $1,984. However, delayed retirement credits do not affect spousal benefits, so as soon as Peter files at seventy, Mary Jane would also file (at age sixty-eight) for her maximum benefit of $800, so their highest possible combined monthly check is $2,784.[51]

When it comes to your Social Security benefits, you obviously will want to consider whether a monthly check based on a fraction of your spouse's earnings will be comparable to or larger than your own earnings history.

Divorced Spouses

There are a few considerations for those of us who have gone through a divorce. If you 1) were married for ten years or more *and* 2) have since been divorced for at least two years *and* 3) are unmarried *and* 4) your ex-spouse qualifies to begin Social Security, you qualify for a spousal benefit based on your ex-spouse's earnings history at FRA. A divorced spousal benefit is different from the married spousal benefit in one way: You don't have to wait for your ex-spouse to file before you can file yourself.[52]

For instance, Charles and Moira were married for fifteen years before their divorce, when he was thirty-six and she was forty. Moira has been remarried for twenty years, and although

[51] Social Security Administration. 2024. "Social Security Benefits" https://www.ssa.gov/OACT/quickcalc/spouse.html#calculator
[52] Social Security Administration. 2024. "Benefits For Your Family" https://www.ssa.gov/benefits/retirement/planner/applying7.html

Charles briefly remarried, his second marriage ended after a few years. Charles' benefits are largely calculated based on his many years of volunteering in schools, meaning his personal monthly benefit is close to zero.

Although Moira has deferred her retirement (opting to delay benefits until she is seventy), Charles can begin taking benefits calculated from Moira's work history at FRA as early as sixty-two. However, he will also have the option of waiting until FRA to collect the maximum, or 50 percent of Moira's earned monthly benefit at her FRA.

Widowed Spouses

If your marriage ended with the death of your spouse, you might claim a benefit for your spouse's earned income as their widow/widower called a survivor's benefit. Unlike spousal benefits or divorced benefits, if your spouse dies, you can claim their full benefit. Also, unlike spousal benefits, you can begin taking income when you turn sixty if you need to. However, as with other benefit options, your monthly check will be permanently reduced for withdrawing benefits before FRA.

If your spouse began taking benefits before they died, you can't delay withdrawing your survivor's benefits to get delayed credits. The Social Security Administration maintains you can only get as much from a survivor's benefit as your deceased spouse might have received had they lived.[53]

Taxes, Taxes, Taxes

With Social Security — as with everything — it is important to consider taxes. It may be surprising, but your Social Security benefits are not tax-free. Despite having been taxed to accrue those benefits in the first place, you may have to pay Uncle Sam income taxes on up to 85 percent of your Social Security.

[53] Social Security Administration. 2024. "Receiving Survivors Benefits Early" https://www.ssa.gov/planners/survivors/survivorchartred.html

The Social Security Administration figures these taxes using what they call "the provisional income formula." Your provisional income formula differs from the adjusted gross income you use for your regular income taxes. Instead, to find out how much of your Social Security benefit is taxable, the Social Security Administration calculates it this way:

Provisional Income = Gross Income + Nontaxable Interest + ½ of Social Security

See that piece about nontaxable interest? That generally means interest from government bonds and notes. It surprises many people that although you may not pay taxes on those assets, their income will count against you when it comes to Social Security taxation.

Once you have figured out your provisional income (also called "combined income"), you can use the following chart to figure out your Social Security taxes.[54]

54 Julia Kagan. Investopedia. October 8, 2022. "Provisional Taxes: What They are and how They Work"
https://www.investopedia.com/terms/p/provisional-income.asp

Taxes on Social Security		
Provisional Income = Gross Income + Nontaxable Interest + ½ of Social Security		
If you are ___ and your provisional income is___, then ...		Uncle Sam will tax ___ of your Social Security
Single	Married, filing jointly	
Less than $25,000	Less than $32,000	0%
$25,000 to $34,000	$32,000 to $44,000	Up to 50%
More than $34,000	More than $44,000	Up to 85%

55

Many taxpayers aged sixty-five and older received an additional tax break in the "One Big Beautiful Bill" in the form of a new $6,000 tax deduction, effective for the 2025 tax year. To qualify for the deduction, you must be at least sixty-five years old by the end of the tax year. For individuals, the deduction starts to phase out when modified adjusted gross income (MAGI) exceeds $75,000 and is completely eliminated when MAGI exceeds $175,000. If you're married and filing a joint tax return, your spouse can also claim the deduction if they're sixty-five or older. For those couples, the phase-out begins at $150,000 MAGI, and the deduction is eliminated at $250,000.[56]

The maximum deduction is $6,000 per eligible taxpayer. For married couples filing jointly, the maximum deduction is $12,000 if both people are age sixty-five or older. It's important

---

55 Ibid.
56 Kelley R Taylor. Kiplinger. June 17, 2025. "$6,000 'Bonus' Tax Deduction Approved for Those Age 65 and Older" https://www.kiplinger.com/taxes/senate-seeks-bigger-tax-break-for-retirees-over-65

to note that this provision is temporary. It will only be available from 2025 through 2028 and will supplement, but not replace, the existing extra standard deduction available to older adults.

The new deduction might extend the opportunity to perform Roth conversions at lower tax brackets by reducing your taxable income. This is especially advantageous for individuals who haven't started receiving Social Security benefits, as their overall taxable income may be lower, allowing for more tax-efficient Roth IRA conversions.

What exactly is MAGI? It's a key financial metric used to determine eligibility for various tax benefits and government programs in the United States, such as premium tax credits, Medicaid, and contributions to Roth IRAs. It starts with your adjusted gross income (AGI), which is your total income minus specific deductions like student loan interest or retirement contributions. MAGI then adds back certain deductions, such as foreign earned income exclusions or tax-exempt interest, to provide a more comprehensive view of your income. While MAGI is not explicitly listed on tax forms, it plays a crucial role in assessing your financial standing for tax-related purposes. As an example, the MAGI limits for Roth contributions follow.

Filing Status	MAGI Limit for Full Contribution	MAGI Limit for Partial Contribution	Not Eligible if MAGI is Over
Single Filers	Less than $150,000	$150,000 - $165,000	$165,000
Married Filing Jointly	Less than $236,000	$236,000 - $246,000	$246,000

[57]

[57] Jason Fernando. Investopedia. February 11, 2025. "Modified Adjusted Gross Income (MAGI): Calculating and Using It" https://www.investopedia.com/terms/m/magi.asp

Provisional income complexities and the senior bonus are both reasons why working with financial advisors and tax professionals may benefit you. They can help you look at your entire financial picture to make your overall retirement plan as tax-efficient as possible — including your Social Security benefit.

To help a couple make their Social Security benefits more tax efficient, we first determine their adjusted gross income. Even though it sounds complicated, it really isn't. It has to do with their provisional income, which is super easy to understand using our Social Security maximization software.

Provisional income is 50 percent of their Social Security. Then, 100 percent of all other income is added, excluding Roth IRAs and certain types of life insurance. That number is then applied to their income brackets to determine whether Social Security will be taxed, and by how much.

This all has to do with reportable, taxable income, so planning before retirement can be beneficial here as it gives us a chance to maybe contribute money into Roth IRAs or certain types of savings accounts to generate lower income.

Also, if you retire early, before sixty-five, if we can keep your income low, you could get subsidized health care. It's all about being proactive.

Working and Social Security: The Earnings Test

If you haven't reached FRA but you started your Social Security benefits and are still working, things get a little hairy.

Because you have started Social Security payments, the Social Security Administration will pay out your benefits (at that reduced rate, of course, because you haven't reached your FRA). Yet, because you are working, the organization must also withhold from your check to add to your benefits, which you are already collecting. See how this complicates matters?

To address the situation, the government has what is called the earnings test. For 2025, you can earn up to $23,400 without it affecting your Social Security check if you're younger than full retirement age. But, for every $2 you earn past that amount, the Social Security Administration will withhold $1. The earnings test loosens in the year of your FRA; if you are reaching FRA in 2025, you can earn up to $62,160 before you run into the earnings test, and the government only withholds $1 for every $3 past that amount.[58]

The month you reach FRA, you are no longer subject to any earnings withholding. For instance, if you are still working and will turn sixty-seven on December 31, 2025, you would only have to worry about the earnings test until December, and then you can ignore it entirely. Keep in mind, the money the government withholds from your Social Security benefits while you are working before FRA will be tacked back onto your benefits check after FRA.[59]

Railroad Retirement Benefits

The Railroad Retirement Act was established in 1934 to address concerns about existing pension programs' ability to provide former railroad employees with old-age benefits.[60] The Act continues to provide benefits to retired and disabled workers, and their dependents, based on their length of employment in the industry. Although there are similarities to Social Security, there are considerable differences, which include payment amounts, eligibility age, and taxation obligations.

---

[58] Rachel Christian. Bankrate. October 24, 2024. "Social Security benefits in 2025: 5 big changes retirees should plan for" https://www.bankrate.com/retirement/social-security-benefits-changes-in-2025/
[59] Social Security Administration. 2024. "Receiving Benefits While Working" https://www.ssa.gov/benefits/retirement/planner/whileworking.html
[60] U.S. Railroad Retirement Board. January 2024. "Agency Overview" https://www.rrb.gov/OurAgency/AgencyOverview

Like Social Security, Railroad Retirement Benefits (RRB) are funded from payroll taxes of current employees and employers. Also, both types of benefits are received by retirees as a monthly check. RRBs use the same formula to calculate COLAs as Social Security.

The differences between the two retirement programs are intricate. The average monthly RRB payment is more generous than Social Security because railroad workers pay higher taxes into the program. Another major difference is the age at which railroad workers are eligible to begin collecting benefits: A railroad worker with thirty or more years of service is eligible for full benefits at age sixty without a reduction.

The taxation of RRBs is more complex than Social Security payments. To determine the tax, RRBs are broken down into two components:

- Tier I benefits resemble Social Security, a private pension, or a combination of both
- Tier II benefits are similar to a private pension[61]

The portion of the Tier I benefit equivalent to Social Security is taxed the same way as Social Security benefits, but the portion not equivalent is fully taxable. Regarding the Tier II, a portion is always taxable and subject to ordinary income tax rates.[62]

Using our Sustainable Retirement Plan and our Social Security Maximization Analysis, we can test when it makes the most sense for each spouse to begin taking Social Security or railroad retirement Social Security. This also helps us determine how to take Social Security income, whether it's a

---

[61] Kurt Woock. NerdWallet. February 7, 2024. "Railroad Retirement Board: What It Is, How It Works" https://www.nerdwallet.com/article/investing/social-security/what-is-the-railroad-retirement-board

[62] True Tamplin. Finance Strategists. September 7, 2023. "Is Railroad Retirement Income Taxable?" https://www.financestrategists.com/retirement-planning/retirement-income-planning/is-railroad-retirement-income-taxable/

primary benefit, a spousal benefit, or other options that make sense for their unique situations.

CHAPTER 6

401(k)s, IRAs, and Roth IRAs

H ave you heard? Today's retirement is not your parents' retirement. You see, back in the day, it was pretty common to work for one company for the vast majority of your career and then retire with a gold watch and a pension.

The gold watch was a symbol of the quality time you had put in at that company, but the pension was more than a symbol. Instead, it was a guarantee — as solid as your employer — that they would repay your hard work with a certain amount of income in your old age. Did you see the caveat there? Your pension's guarantee was *as solid as your employer*. The problem was, what if your employer went under?

Companies that failed couldn't pay their retired employees' pensions, leading to financial challenges for many. Beginning in 1974 with Congress' passage of the Employee Retirement Income Security Act, federal legislation and regulations aimed at protecting retirees were everywhere. One piece of legislation included a relatively obscure section of the Internal Revenue Code, added in 1978 — Section 401(k), to be specific.

IRC section 401, subsection k, created tax advantages for employer-sponsored financial products, even if the main contributor was the employee themselves. Over the years, more employers took note, beginning an age of transition away from pensions and toward 401(k) plans. A 401(k) is a retirement account with certain tax benefits and restrictions on the investments or other financial products inside of it.

Essentially, 401(k)s and their individual retirement account (IRA) counterparts are "wrappers" that provide tax benefits around assets; typically, the assets that compose IRAs and 401(k)s are mutual funds, stock and bond mixes, and money market accounts. However, IRA and 401(k) contents are becoming more diverse these days, with some companies offering different kinds of annuity options within their plans.

Where pensions are defined-*benefit* plans, 401(k)s and IRAs are defined-*contribution* plans. The one-word change outlines the basic difference. Pensions spell out what you can expect to receive from the plan but not necessarily how much money it will take to fund those benefits. With 401(k)s, an employer sets a standard for how much they will contribute (if any), and you can be certain of what you are contributing. Still, there is no outline for what you can expect to receive in return for those contributions.

Modern employment looks very different. A 2022 survey by the Bureau of Labor Statistics determined U.S. workers stayed with their employers for a median of 4.1 years. Workers aged fifty-five to sixty-four had a little more staying power and were most likely to stay with their employer for about ten years.[63] Participation in 401(k) plans appears solid. In a study it conducted, Vanguard reported a record plan participation rate of 83 percent in 2022. Plans with automatic enrollment drew a 93 percent participation rate.[64]

Those statistics make it clear that 401(k) plans have replaced pensions at many companies and, for that matter, a gold watch.

Although pensions aren't as prevalent these days, it's great if you have one since they provide guaranteed income to the owner and maybe the surviving spouse as long as the pension is solvent.

---

[63] U.S. Bureau of Labor Statistics. September 22, 2022. "Employee Tenure Summary" https://www.bls.gov/news.release/tenure.nr0.htm

[64] Vanguard. 2023. "How America Saves 2023" https://institutional.vanguard.com/content/dam/inst/iig-transformation/has/2023/pdf/has-insights/how-america-saves-report-2023.pdf

Often, you have a choice of taking the pension in a lump sum or in monthly installments. If you take your pension in monthly installments, then you have another source of guaranteed income in addition to Social Security. This way, you can withdraw less from your other assets to generate your net monthly income goal.

There are several things to consider with pensions.

Many pensions are underfunded today, which is one thing to consider prior to taking a pension in monthly income installments. It may be better to take the pension in a lump sum.

If a lump sum is available, conduct a pension maximization review to determine if it makes more sense to do monthly installments or a lump sum. Everyone's situation is unique.

Finally, if you're taking your pension in monthly installments, are you taking the life-only option, which means at your death, the pension stops? Or, are you taking a reduced benefit so that at your death, a percentage of your pension is paid to your surviving spouse? You need to know the answer to this question to accurately run a Sustainable Retirement Plan.

Sometimes it's smart to take a reduced pension to enable a surviving spouse to inherit the account. However, if that spouse dies first, the surviving spouse can't name a new beneficiary. Also, it's important to note that the spouse will continue to receive the reduced amount instead of the full amount.

So what should you do? It really depends on several factors, some of which include:

- How much you have in other assets and whether they are tax-deferred, taxable, or tax-free assets
- Whether you're married
- How much you are going to receive from Social Security
- How long you expect you might live.

I believe you need to test these different strategies with an advisor to run the numbers and determine the best strategies for you.

If there is anything to learn from this paradigm shift, it's that you must look out for yourself. Whether you have worked for a company for two years or twenty, you still have to look out for your best interests. That holds doubly true when it comes to preparing for retirement. If you are one of the lucky ones who still has a pension, good for you. But for the rest of us, it is likely a 401(k) — or possibly one of its nonprofit- or government-sector counterparts, a 403(b) or 457 plan — is one of your biggest assets for retirement.

Some employers offer incentives to contribute to their company plans, like a company match. On that subject, I have one thing to say: *Do it!* Nothing in life is free, as they say, but a company match on your retirement funds is about as close to free money as it gets. If you can make the minimum to qualify for your company's match at all, go for it.

Now, it's likely that during our working years, we mostly "set and forget" our 401(k) funding. Because it is tax-advantaged, your employer is taking money from your paycheck — before taxes — and putting it into your plan for you. Maybe you were able to pick a selection of investments, or maybe your company only offers one choice of investment in your 401(k). Either way, while you are gainfully employed, your most impactful decision may just be the decision to continue funding your plan in the first place. But when you are ready to retire or move jobs, you have choices to make requiring a little more thought and care.

When you are ready to part ways with your job, you have a few options:

- Leave the money where it is
- Take the cash (and pay income taxes and perhaps a 10 percent additional federal tax if you are younger than age fifty-nine-and-one-half)
- Transfer the money to another employer plan (if the new plan allows)
- Roll the money over into a self-directed IRA

Now, these are just general options. You will have to decide — hopefully with the help of a financial professional — what's right for you. For instance, 401(k)s are typically pretty closely tied to the companies offering them, so when changing jobs, it may not always be possible to transfer a 401(k) to another 401(k). Leaving the money where it is may also be out of the question — some companies have direct cash payout or rollover policies once someone is no longer employed.

Also, remember what we mentioned earlier about how we change jobs more often these days? That means you likely have a 401(k) with your current company, but you may also have a string of retirement accounts trailing you from other jobs.

My team does a great job of helping clients determine their assets, how they are taxed, the benefit of those assets, and when to make withdrawals from those as part of the process of refining their Sustainable Retirement Plan when they become clients.

However, we can only help with the information we know.

Sadly, although understandably, people can lose track of pensions and retirement accounts they have at companies after leaving them.

That's money they could have as monthly income or lump-sum payouts. That's money that could make a difference in when they can retire or how much they can spend in retirement.

You've got to review the places you have worked in the past. If you're not sure if you had a company retirement plan or pension, then contact that company's HR department to determine if you've left money behind. You might be pleasantly surprised to find newfound money and opportunities that could help with your retirement.

You may wonder if you should put all your money into one account. It may be simpler to have all your assets in one place, but that does not mean it's better. Typically, it's smarter to diversify your investments. If possible, diversify not only among various stocks, bonds, mutual funds, and exchange-traded funds but also try to diversify with different ways that money would be taxed.

You have three basic buckets of money:

- Money that is taxed as regular income, where you receive a 1099, such as interest in checking, savings,

CDs, pension income, dividends, short-term capital gains, and those types of investments.

- Investments that are tax deferred. This could be IRAs, 401(k)s, 403(b)s, 457 plans, and TSP plans, where you deducted the money going into the plan, and you will now pay taxes on all the money when it is withdrawn.

- Tax-free accounts like municipal bond interest (this is counted against you when determining if your Social Security is subject to tax), Roth IRAs, and certain types of life insurance when used appropriately.

By having these three buckets of money, your advisor should be able to blend distributions from these accounts to achieve the best tax result for you now and in the future. I love doing this part of the planning for our clients. I hate taxes, so finding ways to reduce taxes makes me very happy.

If you can track all your different assets regardless of what they are and how they are taxed, and as long as you can easily modify those accounts, they don't have to be in one place.

We have individuals who have more than one IRA account, but it doesn't always make sense to combine them.

When it comes to your retirement income, it's important to be able to pull together *all* your assets, so you can examine what you have and where, and then decide what you will do with it.

Tax-Qualified, Tax-Preferred, Tax-Deferred ... Still TAXED

Financial media often cite IRAs and 401(k)s for their tax benefits. After all, with traditional plans, you put your money in pre-tax, and it hopefully grows for years — even decades — untaxed. That's why these accounts are called "tax-qualified" or "tax-deferred" assets. They aren't *tax-free!* Rarely does Uncle Sam allow business to continue without receiving his piece of the pie, and your retirement assets are no different. If you didn't pay taxes on the front end, you will pay taxes on the money you withdraw from these accounts in retirement. Don't get me wrong: This isn't an inherently good or bad thing; it's just the way it is. It's important to understand, though, for the sake of planning ahead.

In retirement, many people assume they will be in a lower tax bracket. As referenced in the Taxes chapter, for retirees with healthy balances in tax-deferred assets, their retirement marginal tax rate may be the same or even more than their pre-retirement rate. The timing involved with beginning Social Security or in shifting or converting funds out of tax-deferred assets is of strategic concern because of taxes owed on those assets.

Keep in mind, IRAs, 401(k)s, and their alternatives have a few limitations because of their special tax status. For one thing, the IRS sets limits on your contributions to these retirement accounts. If you are contributing to a 401(k) or an equivalent nonprofit or government plan, your annual contribution limit is $23,500 (as of 2025). If you are fifty or older, the IRS allows additional contributions, called "catch-up contributions," of up to $7,500 on top of the regular limit of $23,500. Those aged sixty through sixty-three can make catch-up contributions up to $11,250. For an IRA, the 2025 limit is $7,000, with a catch-up limit of an additional $1,000.[65] Beginning in 2026, catch-up contributions for individuals with income exceeding $145,000 must be transferred into a Roth IRA.[66]

Because their tax advantages come from their intended use as retirement income, withdrawing funds from these accounts before you turn fifty-nine-and-one-half can carry stiff penalties. In addition to fees your investment management

---

[65]IRS. November 1, 2024. "401(k) limit increases to $23,500 for 2025, IRA limit remains $7,000" https://www.irs.gov/newsroom/401k-limit-increases-to-23500-for-2025-ira-limit-remains-7000

[66] Robert Powell. The Street. September 11, 2023. "Ask the Hammer: Catch-up Contributions Now Permitted Until 2026" https://www.thestreet.com/retirement-daily/ask-the-hammer/catch-up-contributions-now-permitted-until-2026

company might charge, you will have to pay income tax *and* a 10 percent federal tax penalty, with a few exceptions.

The fifty-nine-and-one-half rule for retirement accounts is incredibly important to remember, especially when you're young. Younger workers are often tempted to cash out an IRA from a previous employer and then are surprised to find their checks missing 20 percent of the account value to income taxes, penalty taxes, and account fees.

Many millennials I see in my practice say that while they may be socking money away in their workplace retirement plan, it is often the *only* place they are saving. This could be problematic later because of the fifty-nine-and-one-half rule; what if you have an emergency? It is important to fund your retirement, but you need to have some liquid assets handy as emergency funds. This can help you avoid breaking into your retirement accounts and incurring taxes and penalties because of the fifty-nine-and-one-half rule.

RMDs

Remember how we talked about the 401(k) or IRA being a "tax wrapper" for your funds? Well, eventually, Uncle Sam will want a bite of that candy bar. So, when you turn seventy-three, the government requires you to withdraw a portion of your account, which the IRS calculates based on the size of your account and your estimated lifespan. This required minimum distribution (RMD) is the government's insurance it will collect some taxes from your earnings at some point. Because you didn't pay taxes on the front end, you will now pay income taxes on whatever you withdraw — including your RMDs.

Let me reiterate something I pointed out in the Longevity chapter. Beginning at age seventy-three, you are required to withdraw a certain minimum amount every year from your 401(k) or IRA, or else you will face a tax penalty on any RMD monies you should have withdrawn but didn't — and that's on top of income tax. The SECURE Act 2.0 reduced the penalty to

25 percent (from 50 percent). Timely corrections also can reduce the penalty to 10 percent.[67]

Even after you begin RMDs, you can still continue contributing to your 401(k) or IRAs if you are still employed, which can affect the whole discussion on RMDs and possible tax considerations. The SECURE Act 2.0 raised the RMD age to seventy-three from seventy-two. In addition, the latest legislation stipulates the RMD age will increase to seventy-five for those born in 1960 or later.[68]

If you don't need income from your retirement accounts, RMDs can seem like more of a tax burden than an income boon. While some people prefer to reinvest their RMDs, this comes with the possibility of additional taxation: You'll pay income taxes on your RMDs and then potential capital gains taxes on the growth of your investments. If you are legacy-minded, there are other ways to use RMDs, many of which have tax benefits.

SECURE 2.0 Act provisions

In addition to changes imposed for RMD ages, Secure 2.0 Act also expanded access to retirement savings using different methods. Provisions in the legislation go into effect at different times, ranging from 2023-25.

- Beginning January 2, 2024, plan participants could access up to $1,000 (once a year) from retirement savings for emergency, personal, or family expenses without paying a 10 percent early-withdrawal penalty.
- Beginning January 2, 2024, employees could establish a Roth emergency savings account of up to $2,500 per participant.

---

[67] Jim Probasco. Investopedia. October 20, 2023. "SECURE 2.0 Act of 2022: Overview, Rules, Limits" https://www.investopedia.com/secure-2-0-definition-5225115
[68] Ibid.

- Beginning January 2, 2024, domestic abuse survivors could withdraw the lesser of $10,000 or 50 percent of their retirement account without penalty.[69]
- Beginning January 1, 2023, victims of a qualified, federally declared disaster could withdraw up to $22,000 from their retirement account without penalty.[70]

Permanent Life Insurance

One way to turn those pesky RMDs into a legacy is through permanent life insurance. Assuming you need the death benefit coverage and can qualify for it medically, if properly structured, these products can pass on a sizeable death benefit to your beneficiaries — tax-free — as part of your general legacy plan.

ILIT

Another way to use RMDs toward your legacy is to work with an estate planning attorney to create an irrevocable life insurance trust (ILIT). This is basically a permanent life insurance policy placed within a trust. Because the trust is irrevocable, you would relinquish control of it, but unlike with just a permanent life insurance policy, your death benefit won't count toward your taxable estate.

Annuities

Because annuities can be tax-deferred, using all or a portion of your RMDs to fund an annuity contract can be one way to further delay taxation while guaranteeing your income payments (either to you or your loved ones) later. Of course,

---

[69] Betterment editors. Betterment. February 24, 2023. "SECURE Act 2.0: Signed into Law" https://www.betterment.com/work/resources/secure-act-2

[70] Charlie Pastor. The Motley Fool. February 16, 2023. "Law Opens New Doors for Penalty-Free Retirement Account Distributions" www.fool.com/the-ascent/buying-stocks/articles/law-opens-new-doors-for-penalty-free-retirement-account-distributions

this assumes you don't need the RMD income during your retirement.

Qualified Charitable Distributions

If you are charity-minded, you may use your RMDs toward a charitable organization instead of using them for income. You must do this directly from your retirement account (you can't take the RMD check and *then* pay the charity) for your withdrawals to be qualified charitable distributions (QCDs), but this is one way of realizing some of the benefits of a charitable legacy during your own lifetime. You will not need to pay taxes on your QCDs, and they won't count toward your annual charitable tax deduction limit, plus you'll be able to see how the organization you are supporting uses your donations. You should consult a financial professional on how to correctly make a QCD.

We do a tax analysis to determine how best to give you control over your taxes now and in the future. I believe it's important to reduce your taxes over your lifetime, not just over the next two or three years.

Most individuals are not aware that you must begin taking money out of your retirement-type accounts at seventy-three or seventy-five, depending on when you were born. It's important to have an element of control over how much money you must withdraw at age seventy-three or seventy-five as typically that money is 100 percent subject to tax and could cause your Social Security and other investments to be taxed at higher rates, whether you like it or not.

We attempt to use different strategies, such as Roth conversions, to pay the taxes on a schedule that is best for you. Ideally, this will be while taxes are low in order to reduce your future required minimum distributions and taxation on those accounts.

This may make sense to consider because the only way to control the required minimum distributions that must come out of your accounts is to have less money in those accounts that are subject to tax.

Roth IRA

Since the Taxpayer Relief Act of 1997, there has been a different kind of retirement account — or "tax wrapper" — available to the public: the Roth. Roth IRAs and Roth 401(k)s each differ from their traditional counterparts in one big way: You pay your taxes on the front end. Once your post-tax money is in the Roth account, as long as you follow the rules and limitations of that account, your distributions are truly tax-free. You won't pay income tax when you take withdrawals, so in turn, you don't have to worry about RMDs. However, Roth accounts have the same limitations as traditional 401(k)s and IRAs when it comes to withdrawing money before age fifty-nine-and-one-half, with the added stipulation that the account must have been open for at least five years for the account holder to make withdrawals.

We use our Strategic Roth Conversion Analysis to determine the benefits of a Roth conversion or other tax-reduction strategies in your accounts. Everyone is different, and Roth conversions do not always make sense, but seldom is a Roth conversion a one-time event. Normally, it makes sense to create a Roth conversion strategy to convert money from taxable accounts to tax-free accounts that benefit you the most.

Sometimes, we must tell clients this may not be the best year for them to consider those strategies. It may be better to wait until the year after they retire or the following year to start Roth conversions. In addition, there may well be other solutions available that are better than Roth conversions or that work well with Roth conversions to give you more control over your taxes now and in the future.

Conducting this analysis helps us determine when you should start doing Roth conversions and how much can be converted each year.

I don't believe people really understand how simple it is to determine if a conversion is right for them.

Conversions simply change the timing on when you're paying taxes. You can pay the tax now, and any gains thereafter accumulate tax-free for you and your beneficiaries.

People who don't investigate the opportunities of Roth conversions or other tax-reduction strategies often miss opportunities to save money on their taxes. This directly affects how much they can spend on things that make them happy, such as spending more time with their grandchildren or traveling more. Roth conversions have a direct impact on how much more money people can spend because they pay less in taxes for themselves and their beneficiaries.

We conduct tax-reduction analysis for our clients every year. This is rarely a one-and-done situation.

Taking Charge

As mentioned earlier, the 401(k) and IRA have largely replaced pensions, but they aren't an equal trade.

Pensions are employer-funded. The money feeding into them is money that wouldn't ever show up on your pay stub. Because 401(k)s are self-funded, you must actively and consciously save. This distinction has made a difference when it comes to funding retirement. Vanguard published a study in 2025 detailing that the average 401(k) balance for a person aged fifty-five to sixty-four is $271,320, but the median likely tells the whole story. The median 401(k) balance for a person aged fifty-five to sixty-four is $95,642. Those figures reflect Vanguard accounts in 2024.[71]

There can be many reasons why people underfund their retirement plans, like being overwhelmed by investment choices or taking withdrawals from IRAs when they leave an

---

[71] Vanguard. 2024. "How America Saves 2025"
https://institutional.vanguard.com/content/dam/inst/iig-transformation/insights/pdf/2025/has/2025_How_America_Saves.pdf

employer. Still, the reason at the top of the list seems to be this: People simply aren't participating to begin with.

So, whether you use a 401(k) with an employer or an IRA alternative with a private company separate from your workplace, the most important retirement savings decision you can make is to sock away your money somewhere in the first place.

CHAPTER 7

Annuities

In my practice, I offer my clients a variety of products — from securities to insurance — designed to help them work toward their financial goals. You may be wondering: Why single out a single product in this book?

Well, while most of my clients have a pretty good understanding of business and finance, I sometimes find those who have the impression magic must be involved. Some people assume there is a magic finance wand we can wave to change years' worth of savings into a strategy for retirement income. But it's not as easy as a goose laying golden eggs or the Fairy Godmother turning a pumpkin into a coach!

Finances aren't magic; it takes lots of hard work and, typically, several financial products and strategies to pull together a complete retirement plan. Of all the financial products I work with, it seems people find none more mysterious than annuities. And, if I may say, even some of those who recognize the word "annuity" have a limited understanding of the product. So, in the interest of demystifying annuities, let me tell you a little about what an annuity is.

In general, insurance is a financial hedge against risk. Car owners buy auto insurance to protect their finances in case they injure someone or someone injures them. Homeowners have house insurance to protect their homes in case of a fire, flood, or another disaster. People have life insurance to help protect their finances in case of untimely death. Almost juxtaposed to life insurance, people have annuities in case of a long life; annuities can give you financial confidence by providing consistent and reliable income payments.

The basic premise of an annuity is you, the annuitant, pay an insurance company some amount in exchange for their contractual guarantee they will pay you income for a certain time period. How that company pays you, for how long, and how much they offer are all determined by the annuity contract you enter into with the insurance company.

The Ways You Get Paid

There are several ways for an annuity contract to provide income: annuitization, income riders, partial surrenders, and settlement options for heirs.

Annuitization

When someone "annuitizes" a contract, it is the point where they turn on the income stream. Once a contract has been annuitized, there is no going back. With annuities, if the policyholder lives longer than the insurance company planned, the insurance company is still obligated to pay them, even if the payments end up being way more than the contract's actual value.

If, however, the policyholder dies an untimely death, depending on the contract type, the insurance company may keep anything left of the money that funded the annuity. Nothing would be paid out to the contract holder's survivors. You see where that could make some people balk? Now, modern annuities rarely rely on annuitization for the income portion of the contract, and instead have so many bells and whistles that the old concept of annuitization seems outdated, but because this is still an option, it's important to at least understand the basic concept.

Riders

Speaking of bells and whistles, let's talk about riders. Modern annuities have a lot of different options these days, many in the form of riders you can add to your contract for a fee. The fee typically amounts to 0.1 percent to 1 percent of the contract value per year.[72] Each rider has its particulars, and the types of riders available will vary by the type of annuity contract purchased, but I'll just briefly outline some of these little extras:

- Lifetime income rider: Contract guarantees you an enhanced or flexible income for life
- Death benefit rider: Contract pays an enhanced death benefit to your beneficiaries, even if you have annuitized
- Return of premium rider: Guarantees you (or your beneficiaries) will at least receive back the premium value of the annuity
- Long-term care rider: Provides a certain amount, sometimes as much as twice the normal income benefit amount for a period of time to help pay for long-term care if the contract holder is moved to a nursing home or assisted living situation

This isn't an extensive look, and usually the riders have fancier names based on the issuing company, like "Lorem Ipsum Insurance Company Income Preferred Bonus Fixed Index Annuity rider," but I just wanted to show you what some of the general options are in layperson's terms.

Partial Surrender

Most annuities offer a free withdrawal provision that is often referred to as a partial surrender. An annuity contract typically allows for an annual withdrawal of up to 10 percent, typically,

---

[72] Shawn Plummer. The Annuity Expert. 2024. "Annuity Fees: What You Need To Know" https://www.annuityexpertadvice.com/types-of-annuities/annuity-fees/

of the account value or of the premium originally paid. The option to make this withdrawal, typically without penalty, can be used as a tool to help with your income planning strategies. Keep in mind, the withdrawal is subject to income taxes, and an additional 10 percent IRS penalty if you're under age fifty-nine-and-one-half.

This percentage can be accessed during the surrender period and can be a sound strategy, especially for a client who does not require a regular influx of income provided by a rider. After the surrender value period, the holder of the annuity can access the annuity without losing control of the account value.

I find the partial surrender strategy to often be effective for my clients, particularly if they do not need regular income generated through the use of a rider. A partial surrender allows for the annuity holder to just take out funds when a need arises.

Settlement Options

While any value of an annuity left to beneficiaries upon the annuity holder's death is fairly self-explanatory, there is a point worth raising. Heirs have different settlement options they can consider, including opportunities for lump sums, periodic payments, or specific payouts.

Specific payouts are often based on tax considerations involving a beneficiary or multiple beneficiaries. As an advanced tax planning measure, I have clients who have addressed tax implications with their heirs regarding the most advantageous method for arranging a settlement option that eases any tax burden on the beneficiary.

Types of Annuities

Annuities break down into four basic types: immediate, variable, fixed, and fixed index.

Immediate

Immediate annuities primarily rely on annuitization to provide income. You give the insurance company a lump sum up front, and your payments begin immediately. Once you begin receiving income payments, the transaction is irreversible, and you no longer have access to your money in a lump sum. When you die, any remaining contract value is typically forfeited to the insurance company.

All other annuity contract types are "deferred" contracts, meaning you fund your policy as a lump sum or over a period of years. You give it the opportunity to grow over time — sometimes years, sometimes decades.

Variable

A variable annuity is an insurance contract as well as a security product. It's sold by insurance companies, but only through someone who is also registered to sell security products. With a variable annuity contract, the insurance company invests your premiums in sub-accounts that are tied to the stock market.

This makes it a bit different from the other annuity contract types because it is the only contract where your money is subject to losses because of market declines. Your contract value has a greater opportunity to grow, but it also stands to lose. Additionally, your contract's value will be subject to the underlying investment's fees and limitations, including management fees. Once it is time for you to receive income from the contract, the insurance company will pay you a certain income, locked in at whatever your contract's value was.[*]

---

[*] A variable annuity is sold by prospectus. Carefully read the prospectus before purchasing a variable annuity.

Fixed

A traditional fixed annuity is pretty straightforward. You purchase a contract with a guaranteed interest rate, and when you are ready, the insurance company will make regular income payments to you at whatever payout rate your contract guarantees. Those payments will continue for the rest of your life and, if you choose, for the remainder of your spouse's life.

Fixed annuities don't typically offer significant upside potential, but many people like them for their guarantees and predictability. After all, if your Aunt May lives to be ninety-five, knowing she has a paycheck later in life can be her mental and financial safety net. Unlike variable annuities, which are subject to market risk and might be up one year and down the next, you can easily calculate the value of your fixed annuity over your lifetime.

Fixed Index

To recap, variable annuities take on more risk to offer more possibilities to grow. Fixed annuities have less potential growth, but they protect your principal. In the last couple of decades, many insurance companies have retooled their product line to offer fixed indexed annuities, which are sort of midway between variable and fixed annuities on that risk/reward spectrum. Fixed index annuities offer greater growth potential than traditional fixed annuities but less than variable annuities. Like traditional fixed annuities, however, fixed index annuities are protected from downside market losses.

Fixed index annuities earn interest that is tied to an external market index, meaning that instead of your contract value growing at a set interest rate like a traditional fixed annuity, it has the potential to grow within a range. Your contract's value is credited interest based on the performance of an external market index like the S&P 500® while never being invested in the market itself. You can't invest in the S&P 500® directly, but based on when your contract credits interest to your account (e.g., one year — point-to-point, two years — point-to-point, etc.), your annuity has the potential to earn interest based on the chosen index's performance. The interest is subject to limits set by the company (such as caps, spreads, and participation rates).

For instance, if your contract caps your interest at 5 percent, then in a year that the S&P 500® gains 3 percent, your annuity value increases 3 percent. If the S&P 500® gains 35 percent, your annuity value gets a 5 percent interest bump. But since your money isn't actually invested in the market with a fixed index annuity, if the market nosedives (such as happened during 2000, 2008, 2020, and 2022, anyone?), you won't see any increase in your contract value. Insurance carriers charge Mortality & Expense fees (M&E fees) and may charge additional administrative fees to maintain the insurance policy contract that can lower your contract value. Conversely, there will also be no decrease in your contract value, no matter how badly the market performs. As long as you follow the terms of the contract, you won't lose any of the interest you were credited in previous years.

So, what if the S&P 500® shows a market loss of 30 percent? Your contract value isn't going anywhere unless you purchased an optional rider. This charge will still come out of your annuity value each year, along with M&E fees and possibly administrative fees). For those who are more interested in protection than significant growth potential, fixed index annuities can be an attractive option. When the stock market has a long period of positive performance, a fixed index annuity can enjoy conservative growth. And during stretches where the stock market is erratic and stock values across the board take significant losses? Fixed index annuities won't lose anything due to the stock market volatility.

When we help people with retirement planning, we don't care what tools we use as long as they help solve the goals and objectives of our clients.

If appropriate, we may use certain types of annuities to reduce the risk in our clients' accounts so we can withdraw money from those accounts when our clients' investments are down.

We also may use certain types of annuities to replace some or all of a bond's allocation in our clients' portfolios.

However, annuities are not for everyone, and selecting them needs to be very intentional for everyone's unique needs and goals. There is typically a maximum percentage of an individual's assets I would want allocated in these types of accounts.

Other Things to Know About Annuities

We just explained the four kinds of annuity contracts available, but all of them have some commonalities as annuities.

For all annuities, the contractual guarantees are only as strong as the insurance company that sells the product, which makes it important to thoroughly check the credit ratings of any company whose products you are considering.

Annuities are tax-deferred, meaning you don't have to pay taxes on interest earnings each year as the contract value grows. Instead, you will pay ordinary income taxes on your withdrawals. These are meant to be long-term products, so like other tax-deferred or tax-advantaged products, if you begin taking withdrawals from your contract before age fifty-nine-and-one-half, you may also have to pay a 10 percent federal tax penalty. Also, while annuities are generally considered illiquid, some contracts allow you to withdraw up to 10 percent of your contract value every year. Withdraw any more, however, and you could incur additional surrender penalties.

Keep in mind, your withdrawals will deplete the accumulated cash value, death benefit, and possibly the rider values of your contract.

Again, annuities aren't for everyone, but it's important to understand them before saying "yea" or "nay" on whether they fit into your plan; otherwise, you're not operating with complete information, wouldn't you agree? Regardless, you should talk to a financial professional who can help you understand annuities, dissect your particular financial needs, and show you whether an annuity is appropriate for your retirement income plan.

CHAPTER 8

Estate and Legacy Planning Strategies

In my practice, I devote a significant portion of my time to matters of estate and legacy planning strategies. That doesn't mean drawing up wills or trusts or putting together powers of attorney or anything like that. After all, I'm not an estate planning attorney. But I am a financial professional, and what part of the "estate" isn't affected by money matters?

I've included this chapter because I have seen many people do estate planning wrong. Clients, or clients' families, have come in after experiencing a death in the family and have found themselves in the middle of probate, high taxes, or a discovery of something unforeseen (often long-term care) draining the estate.

I have also seen people do estate planning right: clients or families who visit my office to talk about legacies and ways to make them last, and adult children who have room to grieve without an added burden of unintended costs or stress from a family fractured because of inadequate planning.

I'll share some of these stories here. However, I'm not going to give you specific advice, since everyone's situation is unique. I would advise you to speak with an estate planning attorney for specific advice. I only want to give you some things to think about and to underscore the importance of planning ahead.

You Can't Take It With You

When it comes to legacy and estate planning strategies, the most important thing is to *do it*. I have heard people from clients to celebrities (rap artist Snoop Dogg comes to mind) say they aren't interested in what happens to their assets when they die because they'll be dead. That's certainly one way to look at it. But I think that's a very selfish way to go about things. We all have people and causes we care about, and those who care about us. Even if the people we love don't *need* what we leave behind, they can still be fined or legally tied up in the probate process or burial costs if we don't plan for those. And that's not even considering what happens if you become incapacitated at some point while you are still alive. Having a plan in place can greatly help reduce the stress of those responsibilities on your loved ones; it's just a loving thing to do.

Documents

There are a few documents that lay the groundwork for legacy planning. You've probably heard of all or most of them, but I'd like to review what they are and how people commonly use them. These are all things you should talk about with an estate planning attorney to establish your legacy.

Powers of Attorney

A power of attorney, or POA, is a document giving someone the authority to act on your behalf and in your best interests. These come in handy in situations where you cannot be present (think of a vacation where you get stuck in Canada), or for durable powers of attorney (DPOA), even when you are incapacitated (think in a coma or coping with dementia).

It is important to have powers of attorney in place and to appoint someone you trust to act on your behalf in these matters. Have you ever heard of someone who was incapacitated after a car accident, whether from head trauma or being in a coma for weeks — sometimes months? Do you think their bills stopped coming due during that time? I like my phone company and my bank, but neither one is about to put a moratorium on sending me bills — particularly not for an extended or interminable period. A power of attorney would have the authority to pay your mortgage or cancel your cable while you are unable.

You can have multiple attorneys-in-fact and require them to act jointly.

What this looks like: Do you think two heads are better than one? One man, Chris, significantly relied on his two sons' opinions for both his business and personal matters. He appointed both sons as attorneys-in-fact (AIFs), requiring both their signoffs for his medical and financial matters.

You can have multiple attorneys-in-fact who can act independently.

What this looks like: Irene had three children with whom she routinely stayed. They lived in different areas of the country, which she thought was an advantage; one month she might be hiking out West, the next she could enjoy the newest off-Broadway production, and the next she could soak up some Southern sun. She named her three children as independently authorized attorneys-in-fact, so if something happened, no matter where she was, the child closest could step in to act on her behalf.

You can have attorneys-in-fact who have different responsibilities.

What this looks like: Although Luke's friend Claire, a nurse, was his go-to and attorney-in-fact for health-related issues, financial matters usually made her nervous, so he appointed his good neighbor, Matt, as his attorney-in-fact in all of his financial and legal matters.

In addition to POAs, it may be helpful to have an advanced health care directive (HCD), which is sometimes referenced as a *living will.* This is a document where you have pre-decided what choices you would make about different health scenarios. An advanced health care directive can help ease the burden for your medical attorney-in-fact and loved ones, particularly when it comes to end-of-life care.

When selecting a power of attorney, the most important thing is to choose someone you trust. That could include a child, or children, or maybe a sibling. Almost certainly, the medical representative should be the person physically closest to the couple or individual.

It also may be appropriate to have a financial power of attorney, a general and probably a durable power of attorney, which gives someone the legal authority to act on your behalf.

Also, it is important to determine how that power of attorney can be removed if need be.

I have a tale of two families, both of whom happen to be close to me.

One family utilized strategies by having beneficiaries for IRAs and annuities that enabled them to avoid probate court. They used a POD (payable on death) or TOD (transfer on death) for other accounts, whether they were bank-related or investment-related.

In Indiana, a personal home can be transferred through transfer on death, which also avoids probate court.

So, in this case, 100 percent of the assets were transferred to the named beneficiary without probate court or hassle. Most of the transfers were within three to four weeks.

In this case, the transference was so well crafted that the estate had to be opened and funded from some of the POD and TOD accounts to pay out to other individuals who were listed in the will. In other words, there was no money left in the estate as 100 percent of it bypassed probate. Probate typically delays payouts. It's also subject to being contested and could have additional legal and tax fees.

Probate by itself is not bad. The process makes sure beneficiaries can't inherit debt.

An individual could use what's called an unsupervised estate where they don't get the courts involved with probatable assets, which typically doesn't involve a great deal more time unless one of the beneficiaries wants the estate to be overseen by a court.

In the case of the second family, one spouse died at eighty-five, and the survivor was eighty-four. This estate was not well organized, and the surviving spouse really did not fully understand what was left or even where to find the documents. This caused undue anxiety and stress upon the survivor and her children, who had tried to piece the bank accounts, investments accounts, IRAs, pensions, and Social Security together to make sure the survivor had adequate income and confidence that her assets would last a lifetime.

They are still, after five months, trying to put all the pieces together. The decedent had two separate pensions. They are still not certain if the surviving spouse will receive any money from the pension, get half of it, or all of it.

So, taking the time to make sure everything is in order when the first and second spouses pass away may take time and money now but will save time, money, and stress later.

Finally, another negative of probate court is everything is public; therefore, any dirty laundry could be publicly exposed.

Wills

Perhaps the most basic document of legacy planning, a will is a legal document wherein you outline your wishes for your estate. When it comes to your estate after your death, having a will is the foundation of your legacy. Without one, your loved ones are left behind to guess what you would have wanted, and the court will likely split your assets according to the state's probate laws. As far as anyone knows, maybe that's exactly what you wanted, right? Because even if you told your nephew he could have your car he's been driving, if it's not in writing, it still might go to the brother, sister, son, or daughter to whom you aren't speaking.

However, it may not be enough just to have a will. Even with a will, your assets will be subject to probate. Probate is what we call the state's process for determining a will's validity. A judge will go through your will to question if it conflicts with state law, if it is the most up-to-date document, if you were mentally competent at the time it was in order, etc. For some, this is a quick, easily resolved process. For others, particularly if someone steps forward to contest the will, it may take years to settle, all the while subjecting the assets to court costs and attorney's fees.

One other undesirable piece of the probate process is that it is a public process. That means anyone can go to the courthouse, ask for copies of the case, and discover your assets. They can also see who is slated to receive what and who is disputing.

Without a power of attorney or a clear, properly written will, a public probate battle can be painful for all involved.

Take the case of Aretha Franklin. Following the singer's 2018 death, her family didn't think she had a will. Then they discovered two: one under a couch cushion and an earlier one in a cabinet. Neither had been professionally prepared.

Two of her sons favored the will under the couch cushion. Another son favored the more official-looking document in the cabinet, but a Michigan court ruled the notebook found in the couch, the most recent one Franklin had written, stood.

The case made national, and probably beyond, headlines. It was an embarrassing, likely painful episode for the sons who'd already lost their mother, and it didn't have to be.

Details matter. If you ever update your will or write a new one, you need to use the words "this supersedes all other wills." Also, make sure your attorney or financial advisor has a copy of your most recent will, trust, powers of attorney, and medical representative documents and that your power of attorney or executor knows where the documents exist.

Why not make it easy on those you love who will inherit your estate?

I also strongly recommend that all documents be notarized so it is clear that this was your signature and witnessed by someone else.

It's also important to remember beneficiary designations trump wills. So, that large life insurance policy? What if, when you bought it fifteen years ago, you wrote your ex-husband's name on the beneficiary line? Even if you stipulate otherwise in your will, the company that holds your policy will pay out to your ex-spouse. Or how about the thousands of dollars in your IRA you dedicated to the children thirty years ago, but one of your children was killed in a car accident, leaving his wife and two toddlers behind? That IRA is going to transfer to your remaining children, with nothing for your daughter-in-law and grandchildren.

That may paint a grim portrait, but I can't underscore enough the importance of working with a skilled estate planning attorney to keep your will and beneficiary designations up to date as your life changes.

As a final gift to your children, you may want to reduce potential taxes they'll have to pay on their inheritance. If that's the case, you don't want the bulk of those assets to be in accounts that have yet to be taxed.

Given enough time, with the help of a qualified attorney, we can likely structure your estate so that your children may pay virtually nothing in taxes.

You can pay some taxes immediately and reposition some other assets by taking capital losses to get your children as much money as possible with as little tax and hassle as possible.

If some of your assets are through life insurance, that can help pay a tax-free benefit to your children, which can help pay some of the taxes that might remain.

Unfortunately, a lot of times, we learn folks have no estate planning documents in place, such as wills, power of attorney documents, medical representation, trusts, etc., as they always thought they would get to it eventually or felt it was too complex and simply put it off until seeing an advisor.

As part of our process, when individuals become clients, we address estate issues as well as investments, Social Security, pensions, and anything else that can affect your retirement.

We make certain the estate issues are addressed. This typically takes place at our second Sustainable Retirement Planning meeting, where we build and fine-tune a plan.

We will schedule a meeting either with your attorney or we'll assign an attorney with whom we work that we feel will be best suited for you in your situation.

Then, we meet in our office for a thirty-minute complimentary session to discuss these items with you. At the end of that meeting, if you wish to engage that attorney, the process starts. Our team then follows up to make sure that estate planning is completed.

Trusts

Another piece of legacy planning to consider are trusts. A trust is set up through an attorney who appoints and authorizes a trusted party or trustee(s) to administer the trust (e.g., make decisions, manage the assets in the trust, distribute funds from the trust, etc.) according to the provisions of the trust agreement.

Many people are skeptical of trusts because they assume trusts are only appropriate for the fabulously wealthy. A simple trust will likely cost more than $1,000 if prepared by an estate planning attorney, and fees can be higher for couples.[73] But a trust can help you avoid both the expense and publicity of probate, provide a more immediate transfer of wealth, avoid some taxes, and provide you greater control over your legacy.

---

[73] Rickie Houston. SmartAsset. April 5, 2023. "How Much Does It Cost to Set Up a Trust? https://smartasset.com/estate-planning/how-much-does-it-cost-to-set-up-a-trust

For instance, if you want to set aside some funds for a grandchild's college education, you can make it a requirement that they enroll in classes before your trust will dispense any funds. Like a will, beneficiary designations will override your trust conditions, so you still should be keeping your beneficiary designations on insurance policies, investment accounts (e.g., 401(k)s, IRAs, etc.), and other assets up to date.

Like any financial or legal consideration, there are many options these days beyond the simple "yes or no" question of whether to have a trust. For one thing, you will need to consider if you want your trust to be revocable (you can change the terms while you are alive) or irrevocable (can't be changed; you are no longer the "owner" of the contents).

A brief note here about irrevocable trusts: Although they have significant and greater tax benefits, they are still subject to a Medicaid look-back period. If you transfer your assets into an irrevocable trust in an attempt to shelter them from a Medicaid spend-down, you will be ineligible for Medicaid coverage of long-term care for five years. However, an irrevocable trust can avoid both probate and estate taxes, and it can even help protect assets from legal judgments against you.

Another thing to remember when it comes to trusts, in general, is that even if you have set up a trust, you must remember to fund it. In my more than four decades of work, I've had numerous clients come to me assuming they have helped protect their assets with a trust. When we talk about taxes and other pieces of their legacy, it turns out they never retitled any assets or changed any paperwork on the assets they wanted in the trust. So, please remember, a trust is just a bunch of fancy legal papers if you haven't followed through on retitling your assets.

Taxes

Although charitable contributions, trusts, and other tax-efficient strategies can reduce your tax bill, it's unlikely your estate will be passed on entirely tax-free. Yet, when it comes to building a legacy that can last for generations, taxes can be one of the heaviest drains on the impact of your hard work.

For 2025, the federal estate exemption is $13.99 million per individual and $27.98 million for a married couple, with estates facing up to a 40 percent tax rate after that.[74] In addition, we need to account for various state regulations and taxes regarding estate and inheritance transfers.

In 2026, federal estate exemptions increase to $15 million per individual and $30 million for a married couple.[75]

Another tax concern "frequent flyer": retirement accounts.

Your IRA or 401(k) can be a source of tax issues when you pass away. For one thing, taking funds from a sizeable account can trigger a large tax bill. However, if you leave the assets in the account, there are still required minimum distributions (RMDs), which will take effect even after you die. If you pass the account to your spouse, they can keep taking your RMDs as is, or your spouse can retitle the account in their name and receive RMDs based on their life expectancy. Remember, if you don't take your RMDs, the IRS will take up to 25 percent of your required distribution (10 percent if corrections are made in a timely fashion). You will still have to pay income taxes whenever you withdraw that money. Provisions in the original SECURE Act require anyone who inherits your IRA, with few exceptions (your spouse, a beneficiary less than ten years

---

[74] Kate Schubel. Kiplinger. October 21, 2024. "New 2025 Estate Tax Exemption Announced" https://www.kiplinger.com/taxes/whats-the-new-estate-tax-exemption

[75] Husch Blackwell. July 14, 2025. "Estate Planning and Other Tax Strategies under the One Big Beautiful Bill Act" https://www.huschblackwell.com/newsandinsights/estate-planning-and-other-tax-strategies-under-the-one-big-beautiful-bill-act

younger, or a disabled adult child, to name a few), to empty the account within ten years of your death.

Also — and this is a pretty big also — check with an estate planning attorney if you are considering putting your IRA or 401(k) in a trust. An improperly titled beneficiary form for the IRA could mean the difference of thousands of dollars in taxes. This is just one more reason to work with a financial professional, one who can strategically partner with an estate planning attorney and also a tax advisor to diligently check your decisions.

CHAPTER 9

Women Retire Too

I help men, women, and families from all walks of life on their journey to and through retirement. However, we want to address the female demographic specifically. Why? To be perfectly blunt, women are more likely to deal with poverty than men when they reach retirement.

The overall poverty rate for women slightly exceeds the rate for men, but among those seventy-five years and older, 13.51 percent of women live at the poverty rate compared to 8.82 percent of men.[76]

The topics, products, and strategies I cover elsewhere in this book are meant to help address retirement concerns for men *and* women, but the dire statistic above is a reminder that much of traditional planning is geared toward men. Male careers, male lifespans, male health care. The bottom line is women's career paths often look much different than men's, so why would their retirement planning look the same?

Women often embrace different roles and values than men as workers, wives, mothers, and daughters. They are more apt to take on roles as caretakers, thus women are likely to spend portions of their lives making hard shifts between family and careers. Time out of the workforce means less income accumulation for investments and retirement. Also, non-

---

[76] Statista. September 22, 2022. "Poverty rate in the United States in 2021, by age and gender" https://www.statista.com/statistics/233154/us-poverty-rate-by-gender/

working years count as zeroes when calculating Social Security benefits. Women who strongly value family and community tend to focus on lifetime gifting and legacy funding, sometimes to the detriment of their own lifestyles.

These unique choices, challenges, and hurdles make a solid case that women deserve special consideration from financial professionals. The argument is further promoted by the fact that 69 percent of men in the U.S. age sixty-five and older happen to be married, compared to 47 percent of women in that age classification.[77] Single women don't have the opportunity to capitalize on the resource pooling and potential economies of scale accompanying a marriage or partnership.

Though we work with couples and plan for both individuals, it's particularly important that we specifically address concerns that affect women. That's because 90 percent of the time, meaning almost always, they will be the surviving spouses.

It's crucial to test any retirement plan for a couple by looking at what happens if one spouse dies at, say, eighty-five. Test the results if the surviving spouse lives to 100. If that result doesn't look good, don't worry. It's not too late, because we're not in the future yet. We can make changes today.

In my opinion, women often don't spend as much time on retirement planning as men, and they often have different comfort levels when it comes to risk.

With the first death, a spouse also may want to stipulate some restrictions as far as spending through assets so they're not as subject to potential pleas from family members or friends. This can be done through a power of attorney or a bank trustee.

The surviving spouse then is the one to take care of his or her own long-term care needs. It's important to make clear who the health care representative is and have some kind of long-term-care benefit available to pay for that care.

---

[77] Administration for Community Living. November 30, 2022. "Profile of Older Americans" https://acl.gov/aging-and-disability-in-america/data-and-research/profile-older-americans

Be Informed

With all the couples I've seen, there is almost always an "alpha" when it comes to finances. It isn't always men. For many of my coupled clients, the wife is the alpha who keeps the books and budgets and knows where all of the family's assets are, down to the penny. Yet, statistically, among baby boomers, it is usually a man who runs the books. But as time goes on, it looks like the ratio of male to female financial alphas is evening out, based on my experience speaking with couples.

Because most of the baby boomer alphas are men, there is an all too familiar scene in many financial offices across the country: A woman comes into an appointment carrying a sack full of unopened envelopes. Often through tears, she sits across the desk from a financial professional and apologizes her way through a conversation about what financial products she owns and where her income is coming from. She is recently widowed and was sure her spouse was taking care of the finances, but now she doesn't know where all their assets are kept, and her confidence in her financial outlook has wavered after walking through funeral expenses and realizing she's down to one income.

Often, she may be financially "okay." Yet, the uncertainty can be wearying, particularly when the family is already reeling from a loss. While this scenario sometimes plays out with men, in my experience, it's more likely to be a woman in that chair across from my desk. Although the practice has been leveling more and more in recent decades, for centuries Western traditions held money management down as being "a guy thing." But it doesn't have to be this way. This all-too-common scenario can be wiped away with just a little preparation.

Talk to Your Spouse/
Work with a Financial Professional

While there are many factors affecting women's financial preparation for and situation in retirement, I cannot emphasize enough that the decision to be informed, to be a part of the conversation, and to be aware of what is going on with your finances is absolutely paramount to a confident retirement.

The breakdown regarding couples and finances seems to happen because of a lack of communication. The breakdown often seems to stem from no one other than the financial alpha knowing how much the family has and where. In the end, it doesn't matter who handles the money; it's about all parties being informed of what's going on financially.

There are a lot of ways to open the conversation about money. One woman, Ann, started a conversation with her husband, the financial alpha, by sitting down and saying, "Teach me how to be a widow." Perhaps that sounds grim, but it was to the point, and it spurred what she said was a very fruitful conversation. Couples sometimes have their first real conversation about money, assets, and their retirement income approach in our office. The important thing about having these conversations isn't where, it's when. The best "when" is as soon as possible.

Ann told me that after they got the conversation rolling, she and her husband spent a day — just one part of an otherwise dull weekend — going through everything she might need to know. They spent the better part of two decades together after that. When he died and she was widowed, she said the "widowhood" talk had made a huge difference. She knew who to call to talk through their retirement plan and where to call for the insurance policy.

She said the benefit of the weekend exercise they engaged in some twenty years earlier couldn't have been more apparent than when she ultimately accompanied a recently widowed friend to a financial appointment. Her friend was emotional the whole time, afraid she would run out of money any day. The financial professional ultimately showed the friend that she was financially in good shape, but not before the friend had already spent months worried that each check would exhaust her bank account. That's no way to live after losing a loved one. It was preventable had her deceased spouse and financial professional included her in a conversation about "widowhood."

Spouse-Specific Options

One area where it might be especially important to be on the same page between spouses is when it comes to financial products or services that have spousal options. A few that come to mind are pensions and Social Security, although life insurance and annuity policies also have the potential to affect both spouses.

With pensions, taking the worker's life-only option is somewhat attractive. After all, the monthly payment is bigger. However, you and your spouse should discuss your options. When we're talking about both of you as opposed to just one lifespan, there is an increased likelihood at least one of you will live a long, long time. This means the monthly payout will be less, but it also helps ensure that no matter which spouse outlives the other, no one will have to suffer the loss of a needed pension paycheck in their later retirement years.

While we covered Social Security options in a different chapter, I think some of the spousal information bears repeating. Particularly, if you worked exclusively inside the home for a significant number of years, you may want to talk about taking your Social Security benefits based on your spouse's work history. After all, Social Security is based on your thirty-five highest-earning years.

Things to remember about the spousal benefits:[78]

---

[78] Social Security Administration. 2024. "Benefits For Your Family" https://www.ssa.gov/benefits/retirement/planner/applying7.html

- Your benefit will be calculated as a percentage (up to 50 percent) of your spouse's earned monthly benefit at their full retirement age (or FRA).
- For you to begin receiving a spousal benefit, your spouse must have already filed for their benefits, and you must be at least sixty-two.
- You can qualify for a full half of your spouse's benefits if you wait until you reach FRA to file.
- Beginning your benefits earlier than your FRA will reduce your monthly check, but waiting to file until after FRA will not increase your benefits.

For divorcees:[79]
- You may qualify for an ex-spousal benefit if …
  a. You were married for a decade or more
  b. *and* you are at least sixty-two
  c. *and* you have been divorced for at least two years
  d. *and* you are currently unmarried
  e. *and* your ex-spouse is sixty-two (qualifies to begin taking Social Security)
- Your ex-spouse does not need to have filed for you to file on their benefit.
- Similar to spousal benefits, you can qualify for up to half of your ex-spouse's benefits if you wait to file until your FRA.
- If your ex-spouse dies, you may file to receive a widow/widower benefit on their Social Security record as long as you are at least age sixty and fulfill all the other requirements on the preceding alphabetized list.
  a. This will not affect the benefits of your ex-spouse's current spouse

For widow's (or widower's, for that matter) benefits:[80]

---

79 Ibid.
80 Social Security Administration. 2024. "If You Are the Survivor" https://www.ssa.gov/benefits/survivors/ifyou.html

- You may qualify to receive as much as your deceased spouse would have received if ...
    a. You were married for at least nine months before their death
    b. *or* you would qualify for a divorced spousal benefit (if you were divorced and your ex-spouse dies)
    c. *and* you are at least sixty
    d. *and* you did not/have not remarried before age sixty
- You may earn delayed credits on your spouse's benefit *if* your spouse hadn't already filed for benefits when they died.
- Other rules may apply to you if you are disabled or are caring for a deceased spouse's dependent or disabled child.

Longevity

On average, women live longer than men. Most stats put average female longevity at about two years more than men. But averages are tricky things. An April 2022 report by the World Economic Forum listed the eight oldest people in the world as being all women. They ranged in age from 114 years old to 118 and included two Americans.[81]

It's an exciting time to be a woman, as their potential life paths are vast and less subject to judgment than probably at any point in history. Want to stay at home and raise children? Wonderful! Get a PhD in Astrophysics and work for NASA? Fantastic! Do a combination of both? It's happening! On one hand, women all have unique personalities, goals, ambitions, and passions. However, they share biological and instinctual

---

[81] Martin Armstrong. World Economic Forum. April 29, 2022. "How old are the world's oldest people?"
https://www.weforum.org/agenda/2022/04/the-oldest-people-in-the-world/

traits that, in general, give rise to longer lives. And, on that note, the trend for women to live longer presents longstanding financial ramifications.

Women often can live an unexpectedly long time. With them, the goal is to find balance between saving and spending money to do the things they've always wanted to do.

I once knew a woman who lived almost to 100, and she chose to work until ninety-five. In some ways, I think that helped keep her active and healthy, but in other ways, she missed the opportunity to travel and do what she wanted. The result was she died with a lot of money that she could have used to travel and do other things for fun. Sadly, I believe she died with some regrets.

The key is building confidence through guidance from a planner, spending your money while you still can, and saving enough to have adequate care at the end of your life.

Simply Needing More Money in Retirement

Living longer in retirement means needing more money. Period. Barring a huge lottery win or some crazy stock market action, the date you retire is likely the point at which you have the most money you will ever have. Not to put too grim a spin on it, but the problem with longevity is the further you get away from that date, the further your dollars have to stretch. If you only planned to live to a nice eighty-something but instead live to a nice 100-something, that is *two decades* you will need to account for monetarily.

To put this in perspective, let's say you like to drink coffee as an everyday splurge. Not accounting for inflation or leap years, a $4 cup-a-day habit is $29,200 over a two-decade span. Now, think of all the things you like to do that cost money. Add those up for twenty years of unanticipated costs. I think you'll see what I mean.

More Health Care Needs

In addition to the cost of living for a longer lifespan is the fact that aging — plain and simple — means more health care, and more health care means more money. Women are survivors. They suffer from the morbidity-mortality paradox, which states women suffer more non-fatal illnesses throughout their lifetime than men, who experience fewer illnesses but higher mortality.

Women have been found to seek treatment more often when not feeling well and emphasize staying healthy when older, according to studies. Survival, I believe, is on the side of the woman. However, surviving things (such as cancer) also means more checkups later in life.

A statistical concern for women involves the prospect of long-term care. Long-term care for women lasts 3.7 years on average compared to 2.2 years for men.[82]

Widowhood

Not only do women typically live longer than their same-age male counterparts, but they also stand a greater chance of living alone as they age. Some divorce, separate, or never marry. Among those age sixty-five and over, 33 percent of women live alone compared to 20 percent of men.[83]

I don't write this to scare people; rather, I think it's fundamentally important to prepare my female clients for something that may be a startling *but very likely* scenario. At some point, most women will have to handle their financial situations on their own. A little preparation can go a long way,

---

[82] Lindsay Modglin. SingleCare. January 24, 2024. "Long-term care statistics 2024" https://www.singlecare.com/blog/news/long-term-care-statistics/

[83] Statista. November 23, 2022. "Share of senior households living alone in the United States 2020, by gender" https://www.statista.com/statistics/912400/senior-households-living-alone-usa/

and having a basic understanding of your household finances and the "who, what, where, and how much" of your family's assets is incredibly useful. It can prevent a tragic situation from being more traumatic.

In my opinion, the financial services industry sometimes underserves women in these situations. Some financial professionals tend to alienate women, even when their spouses are alive. I've heard several stories of women who sat through meeting after meeting without their financial professional ever addressing a single question to them.

In our firm, when we work with couples, we work hard to make sure our retirement income strategies work for *both* people. No matter who the financial alpha is, it's important for everyone affected by a retirement strategy to understand it.

We have a specific approach for helping widows financially navigate the loss of a spouse.

First, we let them know that thanks to their previous planning, they can take the time to mourn. Nothing must be changed or done immediately.

Then, we make certain that the power of attorney and beneficiaries are involved as soon as possible, whether it's in person or by phone or video conference. We need everyone to participate in planning the next stage for the survivor. We always recommend as many children as possible be involved in that meeting.

We prepare an outline that identifies the accounts that were impacted by the spouse's death. We review that with the family so that everyone understands any changes or recommendations to make.

It is vitally important that everyone be on the same page and, if at all possible, these decisions not be rushed.

Taxes

One of the often-unexpected aspects of widowhood is the tax bill. Many women continue similar lifestyles to the ones they shared with their spouses. This, in turn, means continuing to have a similar need for income. However, after the death of a spouse, their taxes will be calculated based on a single filer's income table, which is much less forgiving than the couple's tax rates. With proper planning, your financial professional and tax advisor may be able to help you take the sting out of your new tax status.

Caregiving

In addition to the financial burden created by caregiving responsibilities, many women often devote many hours each day to duties such as housekeeping and looking after loved ones. So then, when can women find the time to focus long and hard on financial matters?

Unfortunately, the impact and hardships created by traditional roles for women typically do not account for Social Security benefit losses or the losses of health care benefits and retirement savings. This also doesn't account for maternity care, mothers who homeschool, or women who leave the workforce to care for their children in any way.

I don't repeat these statistics to scare you. In America, about 53 million serve as unpaid caregivers and spend roughly $7,000 annually on out-of-pocket caregiving costs.[84] Yet, I think the emotional value of the care many women provide their elderly relatives or neighbors cannot be quantified. So, to be clear, this shouldn't be taken as a "why not to provide caregiving" spiel. Instead, it should be seen as a call for "why to *prepare* for caregiving" or "how to lessen the financial and emotional burden of caregiving."

Funding Your Own Retirement

For these reasons, women should be prepared to fund more of their own retirements. There are several savings options and

---

84 The Scan Foundation. November 10, 2022. "Family caregivers are unsung heroes" https://www.thescanfoundation.org/the-buzz/family-caregivers-are-unsung-heroes

products, including the spousal IRA. They are like a typical IRA except used by a person who's married. The working spouse must earn at least as much money as is contributed into the IRA.[85] This is something to consider, particularly for families where one spouse has dropped out of the workforce to care for a relative. Also, if you find yourself in a caregiving role, talk to your employer's human resources department. Some companies have paid leave, special circumstances, or sick leave options you could qualify for, making it easier to cope and helping you stay longer in the workforce.

Saving Money

Women likely need more money to fund their retirements. But this doesn't have to be a significant burden. Often, women are better at saving while usually taking less risk in their portfolios. One source identified many ways in which women are crushing this retirement component.[86]

- In a 2021 analysis of five million Fidelity customers over a ten-year period, women's investment rates of return outperformed men by .04 percent.
- Wells Fargo found that women take approximately 82 percent of the risk men take.
- Meghan Railey, co-founder and CEO of Optas Capital, wrote, "While we have found that male clients tend to eagerly invest in the latest asset class everyone is talking about, like cryptocurrency, female clients do not generally jump on the shiny bandwagon."

---

[85] Andrea Coombes. NerdWallet. November 2, 2023. "Spousal IRA: What It Is, How to Open One"
https://www.nerdwallet.com/article/investing/spousal-ira-what-it-is-and-why-you-should-open-one
[86] Lyle Daly. The Motley Fool. February 20, 2024. "Investing for Women: What You Should Know"
https://www.fool.com/research/women-in-investing-research/

- Women do a better job buying and holding quality stocks and avoid impulsive decisions. Staying invested for the long haul is often cited as the most effective investing strategy.
- Women remain calm and are less likely to liquidate their retirement accounts during market volatility.
- Lastly, Vanguard found women are less active investors, logging on to their accounts half as often as men and trading 40 percent less frequently.

With all the hurdles to retirement that are unique to women, it's exciting they inherently have an advantage when it comes to saving. This gives me reason to believe as women get more involved in their finances, families will continue to become more confident about retirement.

CHAPTER 10

Pensions

Pensions were once the foundation of a solid retirement income plan for many. These days, however, pensions are an endangered species even as there are more investment vehicles, insurance options, and financial products available than ever before.

If you don't have a pension, read this paragraph, and then go ahead and skip to the next chapter (I'll save you some time here.) Pensions are typically defined-benefit plans. Our employer pays in however much, and, if we work for that employer for a certain number of years (called the vestment period), we are entitled to a payout based on our salary and work history there.

The benefit is the defined part. It's supposed to be income we can definitively count on in retirement. To supplement our pensions, or in the case of those without a pension, some of us are relying on what I believe are fundamentally unreliable or risk-laden assets, like stocks. As you near retirement, it may be appropriate to consider how you might convert your more volatile assets into a guaranteed source of income.

When I first started in the business, pensions were prevalent. Most people didn't live much past age sixty-five, and they may have had plans that consisted of pensions and Social Security. So, two-thirds of their monthly income came from guaranteed sources. What remained came from money they saved along the way.

This was the case with my dad. He had a sizable pension from railroad retirement and railroad Social Security, which generated most of his household income when he retired at about age fifty-five.

Fast forward to today. Very few companies are starting new pensions. Many have dissolved and paid out their existing pensions. Some pensions are under duress due to being underfunded.

Social Security may only be able to pay only about 78 cents on the dollar by the year 2035.

So, two-thirds of monthly income sources are on possibly shaky ground, which leaves most of the burden on you to accumulate money by yourself for your retirement.

I want to believe that Social Security will be available at its full rate when individuals retire as it is a commitment from the government, but I believe that people need to be prepared in the event there is a reduction in Social Security.

When we conduct our Sustainable Retirement Plan with individuals, where they may start taking Social Security at or near the year 2035, we reduce their Social Security payout to 78 percent just to be safe and conservative. We can make additional adjustments if needed.

If you *do* have a pension, congratulations may be in order! This is the American *dream*! You know, a pension, an engraved watch, and riding out of cubicle life into a hazy sunset like a glorious retirement cowboy ...

Whoa, there. Not so fast. Not to look a gift horse in the mouth, but perhaps we should at least check the shoes on this particular equine. Or, to overuse another metaphor, didn't your mother ever tell you not to put all your eggs in one basket? Diversifying the types of assets you own is one of the key parts of planning your income in retirement. Pensions are no exception. The following are a few items on your checklist to keep in mind if you intend to be a proud pensioner down the road.

Check Funding

For one thing, there is a reason pensions have largely gone out of fashion. How well is your pension funded? Since the heyday of the pension, some companies and governments have neglected to fund their pension obligations, creating a persistent problem with this otherwise reliable asset.

Open records laws make it pretty easy to know which government retirement systems have unfunded pension liabilities. About $4 trillion in assets are collectively managed in the United States through public pension funds. Research indicates more risky investments are tied to many of those funds. The ability to meet commitments can hinge on stock market fluctuations.[87]

Private-sector pensions have not always faced the same level of scrutiny as those administered in the public sector. Still, underfunded pensions in the private sector can also be subjected to potential funding gaps.

Every year, companies with private pension plans must file a Form 5500 with the federal government.[88] If you work for a private company, checking up on your plan's health should be a matter of requesting the most recent Form 5500 from your plan administrator.

Check the Fine Print

In addition to checking your pension's funding, be sure to read the fine print. Just like any other financial contract, each company's pension has unique characteristics and options that

---

[87] Nicole Goodkind. CNN. July 14, 2022. "The market meltdown threatening pensions for millions of Americans" https://www.cnn.com/2022/07/14/investing/pensions-markets-unfunded/index.html
[88] U.S. Department of Labor. 2024. "Form 5500 Series" https://www.dol.gov/agencies/ebsa/employers-and-advisers/plan-administration-and-compliance/reporting-and-filing/form-5500

could affect your retirement. For instance, your employer's plan may address inflation by tying income increases automatically to the national Consumer Price Index, by subjecting increases to a vote of a pension advisory board, or maybe by not even accounting for inflation at all. Similarly, some pensions have a provision to provide additional income in retirement if you become disabled. When you're building a financial strategy, it's important to know what those various options are and how they might affect your income payout.

Spousal Options

If you are married, the fine print should extend beyond the page and into a discussion with your spouse. Typically, a pension has two options: *single* life and *joint* life. A single life pension will pay out for the life of the pension owner. It's a significantly larger monthly check, but a flipside exists. Should the pension owner die first, the remaining spouse will receive no further income from the pension. In contrast, a joint life pension encompasses the lifespan of both spouses. Although they will receive a smaller monthly check, that check won't stop coming until both spouses have died.

By utilizing our Sustainable Retirement Plan, we can test the impact of taking a pension for single life only, which is the highest payout a pension allows.

There's another option where a pensioner can take a reduced amount to ensure that after death, his or her spouse can still get part of that monthly income.

Some individuals cannot afford to not have a survivor income. Every situation is somewhat different.

It could depend on the other spouse's health, genetics, and how much of a reduction in their combined Social Security benefits would take place at the first death as well.

Check Your Trajectory

Another piece of the pension puzzle: Pensions aren't portable. Earlier, I mentioned there is a vesting period required in order to collect your pension. For baby boomers and their parents, this wasn't a problem. They didn't change jobs very frequently, and it wasn't unheard of for someone to work for a single employer for twenty years or more. Yet if you're younger, you may have contributed to a trend that finds Americans working 4.1 years on average for the same employer and holding twelve jobs on average during the course of a career.[89]

This means with each new generation, it gets less likely employees can last through the vestment period to even *qualify* for a pension, much less last long enough to have the company store a significant value for their retirement. So, particularly if you think you will consider a career — or just a company — change before retirement, be sure you're considering the fixed nature of your pension, plus any vesting period you'll have to face at a new company.

Check Your Options

If you have a pension, at some point, you will be faced with the decision of how and when you'll begin taking payouts. *Before* the day you plan to ride off into the sunset, it is important to know the ins and outs of your pension.

What do I mean by "outs" of your pension? Well, as some companies and governments fall behind in their pension funding, one of the easiest ways to offload future obligations is for employers to ask employees to retire early and/or to take their pensions as a lump-sum/one-time payout instead of as guaranteed future income payments. Are you prepared for this

---

[89] Elsie Boskamp. Zippia. February 9, 2023. "21 Crucial Career Change Statistics (2023): How Often Do People Change Jobs?" https://www.zippia.com/advice/career-change-statistics/

possibility? Have you considered what you might do with that money (whether you're better off putting it in another product or sticking with the traditional pension), and have you discussed those things with a financial professional?

Sometimes, retirees can improve upon the payments that they would have received from their current pension by utilizing certain types of annuities to provide that same amount of guaranteed income with more flexibility or a higher amount of income.

We can create a hybrid program where some of the money generates guaranteed income. The remainder is invested in an IRA-type account, which allows for liquidity and potentially unlimited growth. It may be advisable to invest all the money in an IRA-type account that allows for liquidity and a diversified investment portfolio for retirees' unique financial objectives.

Save Elsewhere

Pensions were never meant to be the end-all-be-all of retirement, but with today's funding situation — or *under*funding situation — as a whole, they are no longer the firm foundation of financial preparations they were for older generations. So, no matter how well-funded your employer's pension plan is, you should be socking personal savings away in other places, whether in investments, insurance, or bank products.

Regardless of the particulars of your pension and its place in your financial strategies, these conversations should happen sooner rather than later. My hope for you is during the week before your retirement date, the most stressful decision you have is what kind of cake to serve at your retirement party.

CHAPTER 11

Indexed Universal Life Insurance

M y clients are not typically gamblers. A day at the slots is more likely to give them nightmares than it is to make them eager with dollar signs in their eyes. Many would rather work with at least some guarantees than primarily with stocks and risk-based products, so of course, that often means turning more toward life insurance, and often to a product called indexed universal life insurance — also commonly referred to as fixed indexed universal life insurance.

If you've never heard of that before, I'm not surprised. This life insurance product isn't appropriate for everyone, but I want to take a second to talk about it because, for the right person, it can be a significant product in their financial arsenal.

Insurance: The Basics

If you haven't been casting around in the life insurance pond much, then let's take a second to cover the basics. During our working lives, it's likely we have some kind of basic term life policy, either privately or through our employers. Term life insurance means an individual is protected for a certain period of time — usually ten to thirty years. It typically correlates to a certain amount of wages (if it's an employer's plan) or a coverage amount chosen by the individual (if it's a person's private insurance).

At its most basic, term insurance provides funds for our loved ones and can be used for a number of purposes, including covering funeral expenses or something of that nature. Oftentimes, people will take out more than this. For instance, families with a stay-at-home parent sometimes purchase policies based on the working parent's life to cover years of income, plus the mortgage, etc. Your premium for a term life policy will be based on things like your coverage limit, your age, your health, and the term of the policy.

The older you are, the more likely it is you have health events or other issues that could make it more difficult to obtain term life insurance and the more expensive it is. Some consumers may see this as a disadvantage of term life insurance because they pay into a policy for twenty years. Then, it reaches its "endowment" — the end of the contract term — and there are no additional benefits.

Permanent Insurance

Aside from the basic term life policies many wage-earners hold, insurance companies also have permanent policies, also sometimes referred to as "cash value insurance." With a permanent insurance contract, your policy will typically remain in force as long as you continue to keep it funded (there is an exception for whole life policies, which we'll get to later). A permanent insurance contract has two pieces: the death benefit and cash value accumulation.

Both are spelled out in your contract. As these products gained recognition, people began to realize the products had significant advantages when it came to taxes. I don't want to get too technical, but it really is the technical details that make these policies valuable to their owners. That bit about tax advantages makes permanent life insurance policies attractive to consumers. Not only do they receive an income-tax-free death benefit for their beneficiaries, but they may also be able to borrow against their policy, income-tax-free, if they end up needing the money.

For example, let's say Emma purchases a life insurance policy when she's thirty. She hates the idea of not having anything to show for her premiums over ten to twenty years, so she decides to use a permanent policy. Then, when she's close to fifty, her brother finds himself in dire straits. Emma wants to help, and she's been a diligent saver. The catch is most of her money is in products like her 401(k) or an annuity. These may be products appropriate for her needs, but her circumstances have just changed, and she's looking for ways to help her sibling without incurring significant tax penalties.

But wait ... she has that permanent life insurance policy! She can borrow any accumulated cash value against her policy, free of income taxes. So, let's say she borrows a few thousand dollars from her policy. She doesn't have to pay taxes on any of it. She can pay it back into her policy at any time. Then, let's say Emma dies before she "settles up" her policy (or pays back that loan). As long as she continues to pay premium payments or otherwise keeps her policy adequately funded until she dies, then her beneficiaries will still receive a death benefit minus the policy loan.

Are you with me so far? Here are the central themes on properly structured permanent life insurance policies: tax-free death benefit and income-tax-free withdrawals through policy loans are available as long as the premiums continue to be paid, and a minimum rate of cash value accumulation is guaranteed by the strength of the insurer.

Now, let's dive a little deeper into the two basic categories of permanent insurance on the market: whole life policies and universal life policies.

Whole Life Insurance

With whole life, an actuary in a back office has calculated what a person your age with your intended death benefit coverage, your health history, your potential lifespan — and other minutia — should pay for a premium rate. Depending on how the insurer calculates rate tables, your whole life policy will "endow" at a certain age — ninety, 100, 120, etc. — so there is the risk you could outlive the policy. The death benefit would pay out to you instead of your beneficiaries, which may create unplanned tax consequences.

Nonetheless, to qualify for your whole life policy, you will complete a medical questionnaire and possibly a paramedical exam, and based on that information, an underwriter will place you in one of these actuarial categories to determine your premium rate. One benefit of whole life insurance is the insurance company will credit a certain amount back into the policy's cash value based on your contract's guaranteed rate. Some insurance companies may also pay a dividend back to policyholders at the company's discretion.

Take Emma from the preceding example, and let's consider the scenario if her permanent insurance policy was a whole life policy. When she first purchased the contract, the insurance agent would have been able to tell her what her locked-in premium rate would be. She would pay the same amount, year after year, to keep her contract in force. And she could also calculate her policy's minimum cash value to the penny.

Universal Life Insurance

If whole life is the basic permanent life insurance policy, universal is the souped-up model. It has eight speeds, comes in many colors, and has more options, which means it might take some extra time and research to be thoroughly understood. But this means if it's right for you, it can be even more customizable and fine-tuned to your specific needs.

The major differences:
- Flexible premium
- Increasing policy costs

Let's start with those increasing policy costs. Basically, the internal cost to the insurance company of maintaining your policy will increase over time, like a term insurance policy. Remember how whole life policies have those actuaries at the insurer's office calculating all of that and then determining a set rate for you to pay to cover it all? Well, with universal life, that's part of the flexible premium part. You can decide to pay a premium that will cover your future policy expenses, or you can decide to pay a premium that barely covers your current policy expenses, depending on your circumstances.

That is where these policies have gotten a bad rap in the past. If you purchase a policy and only ever pay the minimum premium required, your policy could lose value to the point that your premium no longer covers your policy's expenses, and then the policy would lapse. That's also why it's incredibly important to work with a financial professional you trust. This financial professional should shoot straight about whether this kind of product would be appropriate for you and make sure you fully understand all the details.

To return to our example of Emma, though, here's how a well-set-up universal life insurance policy could work: Emma, ever the diligent saver, would have paid well over the minimum premium every month. Every time she got a raise or payroll increase, she increased the amount of premium she paid into her policy. With the policy's contractual rate of interest, she had a substantial amount of cash value accumulated in the policy. That way, when she decided to borrow money against the policy to help her brother, she could even afford to decrease her monthly payments for a time, until she was back in a better financial position.

Indexing

Now to the main event: *indexed* universal life insurance (IUL). Like any permanent insurance, an IUL policy will remain in force as long as you continue to pay sufficient premiums, and you can borrow against your policy's cash value, income-tax-free. At their core, IUL policies are universal life insurance policies with flexible premiums. So, how are they different?

If you skim back through some of the other policy details, I covered the ability to withdraw the cash value of your policy without paying income taxes, even on the accumulation. Because of the index part of IULs, that accumulating cash value has the potential to accumulate more. An index is a tool that measures the movement of the market, like the S&P 500® or the Dow Jones Industrial Average. You can't invest directly in an index. It's just a sort of ruler.

With an IUL policy, your cash accumulation interest credits are based on an index, with what is called a "floor" and a "cap" or other limits such as a spread or participation rate. If the market does well, each year your policy can be credited interest on the cash accumulation based on whatever your policy's index is, subject to the cap, spread, or participation rate. If the market has a bad year and the index shows negative gains, your account still gets credited, whatever your contract floor is.

So, for example, let's say your contract cap is 12.5 percent and the floor is 0 percent. If the market returns 20 percent, your contract value gets a 12.5 percent interest credit. The next year, the S&P 500® returns a negative 26 percent. The insurance company won't credit your policy anything, but you also won't see your policy value slip because of that negative performance (although M&E fees and administrative fees will still be deducted from your policy). So, your policy won't lose value because of poor market conditions, but you can still stand to realize interest credits due to changes in an index.

Another opportunity IUL policies present is for a policyholder to overfund the policy cash value in the first five or ten years and then, potentially, not have to pay any more money into the policy, letting the cash accumulation self-fund the policy. However, when overfunding an IUL policy, it is important to understand the policy may become a modified endowment contract (or MEC) if premium payments exceed certain amounts specified under the Internal Revenue Code.

This can happen if a policy has been funded too quickly in its early years. For MECs, distributions during the life of the insured (including loans) are fully taxable as income to the extent there is a gain in the policy over the amount of net premiums paid. An additional 10 percent federal income tax may apply for withdrawals made before age fifty-nine-and-one-half.

So, back to our friend, Emma. If her permanent life insurance policy was an IUL, what might that have looked like? Emma saves, paying well over the mandatory minimum of her IUL policy. Let's assume the market does well for decades. Her policy accumulates a significant cash value. At some point, she stops paying as much in premium, or maybe she stops paying any premium from her own pocket at all because her policy has enough cash value to pay for its own expenses with the insurance company. Then, when her brother needs help, there is enough cash value stored in the policy.

It's important to note that making withdrawals or taking policy loans from a policy may have an adverse effect. You may want to talk to your financial professional to re-evaluate your premium payment schedule if you are considering this option.

If you're reeling just a bit, it's understandable. There's a lot going on with these policies. If you don't take the time to understand the basics of how they work, it's entirely possible to fall behind on premium payments and end up with a policy that lapses. Yet, if you understand the terms of your contract and are working with purpose, an IUL policy could be a powerful cog in the greater mechanics of your overall retirement strategy.

An indexed universal life insurance policy can be a possible replacement for the loss of Social Security income at the death of the first spouse and is a potential alternative to a Roth conversion.

Such a policy also can help equalize an estate. Take someone who has, say, $2 million in farmland and $800,000 in liquid assets. If this person has five children, and one child farms the land and wants to inherit the land, that doesn't leave an equal amount to divide among the other children.

The child who farms the land will get the farm upon the parent's death. However, if there is not enough in liquid assets to give each of the remaining children an equal amount of inheritance, purchasing life insurance to be paid to the other children at the last spouse's death can equalize the inheritance on a tax-free basis.

The other children would be able to accumulate money for later in retirement that, if done properly, can be withdrawn tax-free.

There are many other potential uses for this type of insurance depending on the needs of a family or an estate.

CHAPTER 12

Long-Term Care Insurance

Elsewhere in this book, I've outlined the potential risks longevity poses to your financial health. In fact, you may be tired of hearing it at this point.

Even so, I'd still like to repeat one more time — in case you've forgotten — it's estimated *seven* out of every ten Americans who reach age sixty-five will need long-term care of some kind.[90] Let me ask: If you knew the car you were going to be riding in had a 70 percent chance of having an accident, would you wear your seatbelt?

I have seen individuals forced to make decisions they didn't want to make because they didn't have adequate funds to care for their spouse due to dementia or other health situations.

In many cases, this puts an additional burden on the other spouse, their children, and friends to help provide a level of care for that loved one because additional funds either were not available or, for whatever reason, were not used. It's a sad situation that is avoidable with proper planning.

The bottom line is we need to do a better job of planning for the possibility of long-term care. However, if you think about the current problems plaguing government-run programs such

---

[90] Lindsay Modglin. SingleCare. January 24, 2024. "Long-term care statistics 2024" https://www.singlecare.com/blog/news/long-term-care-statistics/

as Social Security, Medicaid, and Medicare, I think it stands to reason we're probably on our own for the time being.

Elsewhere, I covered the various ways of preparing for our own possible long-term care costs, from self-funding to insurance riders. I'd like to take a moment to expand on what is one of the most comprehensive coverage options: long-term care insurance.

LTCI Basics

The long-term care insurance (LTCI) space has had a bit of a shakeup in the past few years. Many insurers stopped offering LTCI, and the policies remaining are often more expensive. In addition, denials of LTCI applications have risen to the point that 38.2 percent of those between the ages of sixty-five and sixty-nine are rejected. The percentage increases to 47 percent for applicants aged seventy to seventy-five.[91]

Yet, on the other side of the coin are the insurers left in the LTCI space. They have experience and policies that have endured. LTCI may be more expensive for individuals, but that's because they can be more expensive for insurers, and overall, long-term care is just plain expensive, period. It's important to understand that LTCI carriers aren't just making money hand-over-fist with these products. Instead, the carriers who have stopped selling policies were likely carriers who had unrealistic prices and underperforming policies. According to one report, prices have stabilized yet could still be considered expensive to some.[92]

---

[91] American Association for Long-Term Care Insurance. 2024. "Nearly Half Of Oldest Long-Term Care Insurance Applicants Denied"
https://www.aaltci.org/news/long-term-care-insurance-association-news/applicants-declined
[92] American Association for Long-Term Care Insurance. 2024. "2022 Price Index For Long-Term Care Insurance Released"
https://www.aaltci.org/news/long-term-care-insurance-association-news/2022-price-index-for-long-term-care-insurance

While many criticize the use-it-or-lose-it nature of LTCI, it is reasonable to consider that homeowner's insurance, car insurance, term life insurance, and many other types of insurance work the same way. Yes, you are paying into a policy in the hopes you may never use it. But if you must use it, it can provide value well beyond the actual dollars you have paid into it. An average of 358,500 experience a structural home fire every year[93] for the 131.43 million households in the United States.[94] I share those numbers because you have *less than a half percent chance* of experiencing a home fire in any given year. However, most of us would still squirm at the thought of not having homeowner's or renter's insurance to cover fire damage. Paradoxically, while LongTermCare.gov cites that those turning sixty-five stand a 70 percent chance of needing long-term care, only 10 percent of Americans have LTCI.[95]

To purchase LTCI, you have to complete an application that includes a medical questionnaire. Depending on your age and the insurance carrier, you may also need to complete a medical exam. If you qualify, then the insurance company will offer you a policy with certain coverage and pricing based in part on your odds of needing long-term care in the future. The younger you are, the more likely you are to qualify — at a rate that is more likely affordable for you.

LTCI premiums count as medical expenses and may potentially be paid with special tax considerations. For instance, if you are eligible to itemize your medical expenses, LTCI premiums can be itemized. Or, alternatively, you can pay premiums with tax-free money in health savings accounts. The amount you can withdraw tax-free for LTCI premiums depends on your age.

93 The Zebra. January 31, 2023. "House Fire Statistics"
https://www.thezebra.com/resources/research/house-fire-statistics/
94 Veera Korhonen. Statista. November 22, 2023. "Number of households in the U.S. from 1960 to 2023"
https://www.statista.com/statistics/183635/number-of-households-in-the-us
95 HGC Secure. 2024. "Long-Term Care Perceptions & Preparation"
https://hcgsecure.com/independent-research/

If you have an LTCI policy, coverage will typically kick in when you have been medically shown to be unable to perform two or more activities of daily living (ADLs). An ADL is an activity such as bathing, toileting, eating, dressing, grooming, and getting in and out of a bed or chair. These are all things we naturally prefer to do by ourselves. They are markers of our independence and ability to take care of ourselves. Once someone is unable to do some of these things alone, they need long-term help.

So, if you have LTCI, once you reach this point, you will qualify for a daily amount of coverage over a pre-selected time period, depending on the terms of your policy. That money could be used to cover a nursing home stay, in-home care, or community organization care. The benefits will begin after the policy's elimination period, which you choose when you purchase the policy. The elimination period can range from 0 to 180 days, and the shorter the elimination period, the higher the premium.

With LTCI, you can pick and choose facilities or care options according to your standards instead of having the government decide what is best for you.

Long-Term Care Partnership Program

One other significant advantage of LTCI is many plans are eligible for a federal-state government initiative called the Long-Term Care Partnership Program.[96] This program is a joint effort by the federal government and certain states to help individuals decide to choose LTCI protection. It means if you deplete your LTCI coverage and find yourself in a position of having to spend down your assets to become eligible for Medicaid, part or all of your LTCI coverage limit will extend to

---

[96] American Association for Long-Term Care Insurance. 2024. "Long Term Care Insurance Partnership Plans" http://www.aaltci.org/long-term-care-insurance/learning-center/long-term-care-insurance-partnership-plans.php

your assets. Here's what this might look like "in real life" (using, of course, a completely hypothetical person):

Jennifer chooses an LTCI policy to cover up to three years of nursing home care (a little more than the average long-term care stay) in a semi-private room. After several injuries render her unable to dress or bathe herself, Jennifer moves to Winters Retirement Community. Jennifer is not average. Her policy has paid out more than $250,000 on her behalf, and her policy benefits are now exhausted. This puts her in position for a Medicaid spend down. However, because she purchased a policy her state approved in line with the Long-Term Care Partnership Program, instead of having to spend down her assets to the Medicaid requirement and leaving very little for her family to inherit, she is allowed to set aside $250,000 on top of her state's other spend-down exemptions.[97]

LTCI — It's Not Just About You

Aside from the partnership program and possible tax advantages of traditional LTCI, I think perhaps one of the most compelling arguments in favor of preparing for the likelihood of long-term care has less to do with our own personal assets and more to do with others.

What do I mean? Well, I hear from lots of people who think it won't matter. "Oh, by the time I reach the point of needing long-term care, I'll be out of my mind. Who cares who takes care of me and how that happens?"

However, like estate planning, long-term care planning isn't solely about us. In fact, I might argue that the most important piece of long-term care planning isn't about you at all. It's about your loved ones. It's about your spouse, your children, or your

---

[97] American Council On Aging. February 8, 2024. "How Purchasing Long-Term Care Insurance Can Help Medicaid Beneficiaries Protect Their Homes & Assets"
https://www.medicaidplanningassistance.org/partnerships-for-long-term-care/

friends, and how caring for you could impact them if you don't have the necessary resources.

Most caregiving for the elderly happens in people's private homes. One report found that only 11 percent of elderly Americans requiring care services live in a nursing home or assisted living facility.[98] Among other findings:

- Of those surveyed, a mean of nineteen hours a week was provided in care. Among those, about 38 percent had to cut back their hours at their job.
- The average age of an in-home caregiver is forty-nine. Of those providing in-home care, 66 percent are women.

About 1.3 million caregivers are children between the ages of eight and eighteen, with three-fourths of those caring for a parent or grandparent.

We offer long-term care insurance because we believe our clients need to at least have the option of considering whether long-term care coverage would be beneficial to them and potentially their families.

There has been evidence that if it is not at least offered to clients, then children who stood to inherit their assets — and then didn't because the parents used all or most of their money on long-term care — end up suing financial representatives. People actually have won these cases.

We'll offer it, and if people refuse it, we document it.

Because of its benefits for both the policyholder and their family or caregiver, LTCI can be a valuable asset in any retirement plan.

---

98 John Hopkins Medicine. 2024. "Being a Caregiver"
https://www.hopkinsmedicine.org/health/caregiving/being-a-caregiver

CHAPTER 13

Charity

W ills and testaments, trusts, and powers of attorney are all pieces of what we often call legacy planning. But I would be remiss if I didn't address a piece of legacy preparation near and dear to my heart: charitable contributions.

Charity is one of those universal concepts that unites us as human beings. Football players who dedicate their resources to building homes for single moms, communities who help neighbors rebuild after catastrophes, groundskeepers who donate millions from under a mattress to their favorite university, or private donors who put impoverished children through school. These are the stories that inspire us and drive us to be better people.

There are many, many ways to pass money to your favorite charity, university, foundation, or public resource. Some include using qualified charitable distributions with the mandatory withdrawals from your IRA, and others lend themselves to establishing trusts. Whatever your preferred method of charitable distribution, the right financial professional will partner with a qualified tax advisor and/or estate planning attorney to discover how to help you make your contributions in a way that fits well within your own strategy for taxes. They help ensure your contributions are passed efficiently to your intended beneficiary.

Let's look at an example of a couple who had a goal to reduce taxes on their estate when it was transferred to their children. They also were charitably minded. They were able to establish a type of charitable trust where they made a large, lump-sum contribution from their nonretirement-type accounts.

These people didn't expect to take much income from that investment over their lifetimes. They received a sizable deduction on their taxes, which was used to offset taxes due when they converted a large amount of money from a taxable IRA into a tax-free Roth. That meant that they no longer had to take the required minimum distributions from the IRA, which would have been subject to tax.

Then, that account, including growth, could transfer to their beneficiaries with no tax.

This accomplished one of their goals of transferring money efficiently with as little tax to their heirs as possible.

The second goal was to pay the money into the charitable trust, which allows both the principal and interest to be withdrawn to provide income.

They also could control the charitable trust beneficiary and change the beneficiary or beneficiaries of this trust account that would be paid out at their deaths. It's nice to have this control.

For example, if they're giving money to a local college, then the college would be notified that they are the beneficiary.

The school also would know that could change. That's a good incentive for the college to make sure potential donors have good tickets to ball games and other events.

Where to Start?

We've all heard it is better to give than to receive, and science backs this up. Multiple studies show those who give to charity or volunteer experience less depression, lower blood pressure, higher self-esteem, and greater happiness.[99]

It's a common perception, however, that retirees are less inclined to be charitable. It seems like reasoned logic — they're living on fixed incomes, and it's difficult to work charitable giving into conservative strategies designed to protect assets. But this counters the facts. In a recent study, more baby boomers donated to charities than any other generation. On average, the average gift per baby boomer is $1,212.[100]

So, how do we keep up or even increase our retirement donations? Well, as with all the other topics we cover in this book, step one is to build charitable giving into our retirement plans. Advanced planning can help you be sure your donations — at least in the monetary sense — are given in the most tax-efficient and effective way, both for you and the charity to which you contribute.

Planned Giving: Lifetime

When we're talking about charitable contributions, it's important to distinguish between lifetime giving and charitable giving as part of a well-prepared estate plan.

The American tax system has many provisions to encourage charitable giving. I'm sure the reasoning goes something along the lines of, "If we, the people, were naturally able to care for the poor and vulnerable in our own communities through our own means, we collectively would need to pay fewer taxes to support federal aid to those same people." It's a wonderful consideration and one we should all aspire to. But in practice,

---

[99] Jeanne Segal and Lawrence Robinson. HelpGuide.org. February 5, 2024. "Volunteering and its Surprising Benefits" https://www.helpguide.org/articles/healthy-living/volunteering-and-its-surprising-benefits.htm

[100] Duke Haddad. NonProfitPRO. March 11, 2022. "A Look at Generational Giving Donor Trends and Influences" https://www.nonprofitpro.com/post/a-look-at-generational-giving-donor-trends-and-influences

it gets more difficult as tax codes change and shift according to political administrations and other public considerations. Ensuring your charitable contributions are tax-efficient is not a one-time move — it requires yearly analysis.

It's important to remember your charitable giving is most effective when the combined amount of your *itemized* deductions is more than your *standard* deduction. Now, it isn't only charity that counts toward your itemized deductions. There are also medical expenses, mortgage interest, and other taxes such as real estate tax and state income tax. Deductions change year to year, of course, but the IRS usually publishes the following year's charts in November. When you're itemizing deductions, you may typically deduct up to 60 percent of your adjusted gross (pre-tax) income, though in some cases, other limitations apply.[101]

Another thing to keep in mind if you are considering the tax implications of a charitable donation, you must have a receipt, a canceled check, or some demonstrable way of recording the transaction. Specifically, in the event you are audited, you will need a donation acknowledgment receipt from the charity for any cash or non-cash amounts over $250. Additionally, many charitable activities aren't eligible as a tax deduction. Raffle tickets, charity event entrance fees, and those sorts of things are not typically counted as charitable deductions on your taxes. A quick rule of thumb is if you received something in return for your donation, it's not tax-deductible.

Perhaps one of the most crucial things to keep in mind when it comes to the tax implications of charitable giving, however, is "nonprofit" doesn't mean "tax-advantaged." The IRS keeps a long list of organizations that qualify for tax-deducted gifting in the Internal Revenue Code section 501(c)(3). Yet many excellent nonprofits and civic organizations are not 501(c)(3)s. That doesn't mean you shouldn't give to them. Truly, charity is

---

[101] Internal Revenue Service. Dec 5, 2023. "Charitable Contribution Deductions" https://www.irs.gov/charities-non-profits/charitable-organizations/charitable-contribution-deductions

not about tax deductions when it comes right down to it. It just means you shouldn't plan to include it as part of your tax-efficiency strategies.

Again, I would be remiss not to emphasize that these laws and definitions change year to year, so it is important to work with a team of qualified financial and tax professionals who can help you plan for the future and adjust to the times, in addition to verifying whether the charity you are considering is tax-exempt.

While impermanence seems to be a fixture of our tax system, one important aspect of charity tax law was made permanent for the foreseeable future. In 2015, Congress passed a budget deal signed into law by President Barack Obama. Among the provisions of the "Protecting Americans From Tax Hikes Act of 2015," which included this important measure:

- IRA charitable rollovers — at age seventy-and-one-half, owners of traditional IRAs can give up to $108,000 a year to a qualified charity directly from the IRA.[102] This is known as a qualified charitable distribution (QCD).

What makes this deduction so important is a person who uses an IRA to contribute to charity in this way can:

- Be charitable.
- Avoid having their RMDs push them into a higher tax bracket by instead gifting them to those in need.
- Take advantage of the tax-free aspect of a QCD when planning charitable gifting.
- Potentially use the tax break to offset other tax consequences, like the tax on appreciated assets or capital gains.

---

102 IRS. November 14, 2024. "Give more, tax-free: Eligible IRA owners can donate up to $105,000 to charity in 2024"
https://www.irs.gov/newsroom/give-more-tax-free-eligible-ira-owners-can-donate-up-to-105000-to-charity-in-2024

With an allowance for IRA contributions after an individual reaches age seventy-three, QCDs will be adversely affected if a contribution is made to that IRA in the same year a QCD is withdrawn.

If you're over seventy-and-one-half, you can contribute up to $100,000 through a qualified charitable distribution from your IRA to a qualified charity, which eliminates tax on the distribution.

Also, I believe if you're seventy-and-one-half or older, your first charitable payment should come from your IRA accounts because, with today's high standard deductions, many individuals cannot benefit from contributions to charities from a tax standpoint by itemizing.

There are many other tax-reduction strategies, such as Roth conversions, capital gains losses, charitable trusts, wise usage of income sources, and more.

The correct choice is unique to each individual.

Planned Giving: After My Lifetime

For many charities, endowments and legacy gifts are the lifeblood that keeps them going. And for many of us, a large final gift is an excellent way to continue a legacy of giving into perpetuity. The financial reasons for final charitable gifts, much like the annual contributions we often give, are many and (mostly) tax-based. A large final gift can be a good way to offload highly appreciated assets, allowing our favorite charities to experience the full use of an asset without us having to pay out a sizable tax bill.

Many charities have gone to great lengths to make this an attractive option, with some having preferences for certain donation types and strategies. For instance, many public entities, such as libraries and schools, have foundations to collect most of the donations and do major fundraising. Churches and universities often have special projects and intentional funding that stems from sizable endowments.

There are many financial vehicles to help you meet your charitable goals and give you benefits during your lifetime as well — from permanent life insurance policies to charitable trusts and charitable annuities. That's why it's important to plan ahead and work with a goal in mind. If you have some idea of what end you want to achieve, it can be easier to find the estate attorneys, tax professionals, and financial professionals who will be best qualified to help.

Non-Monetary Charitable Contributions

Ultimately, aside from the tax breaks, the good feeling, and the name on a park bench you might receive, your charitable contributions aren't about what you "get" in return. This is one other reason we should plan ahead for our good works; it's about doing the right thing.

Volunteering is one great, non-monetary way to support the charities and causes we believe in. As I noted earlier, research shows retirees who are active and engaged volunteers in their communities often have a better sense of purpose and report more happiness than those who aren't. In volunteering, we have a reason to get up in the morning, and we meet new people and make friends. These are all things that may previously have stemmed from your nine-to-five workday but tend to fall by the wayside after leaving the workforce, making this consideration even more important.

When our youngest son, Joshua, was diagnosed with cancer in sixth grade, we contacted Make-A-Wish, and the organization provided him, his mother, one of his sisters, and me with an all-expense paid trip to see the stars of "Mythbusters." It was his favorite TV show. The experience gave him and other Make-A-Wish families encouragement to fight their battles.

After that, friends and even some of my clients started hosting events to raise money for Make-A-Wish.

Joshua attends pharmacy school, and after he graduates, he plans to give back by serving missions through Samaritan's Purse.

We have other clients who donate time to multiple charities, such as Habitat for Humanity and local churches, simply to give back for all the blessings they have and will receive over their lifetimes.

Kathy and I tithe first as we believe it's important to give to God what is God's.

In addition, we support several ministries, missions, and a group called Community Worship Arts, where I'm a board member for Christian-based plays that encourage individuals in tough economic and financial times to give them hope. We found that theater allows individuals to feel and sense emotions based upon the actors and actresses involved. They put themselves in those individuals' positions, realizing that even though things may appear to be bad, there's always a good ending to that story.

Our families are one way we leave a legacy. But charitable giving — with our time, our talents, and our treasure — allows us to extend our legacies even further, beyond passing on Grandpa's nose or Grandma's ticklish feet.

CHAPTER 14

Finding a Financial Professional

A t this point, you may be feeling overwhelmed with information. Or perhaps you've learned some key points about investing for your future and are excited to get started.

More than likely, you're feeling a bit of both. That's where my team and I can help.

One common theme I've found is that the people who retire well are educated — educated about their retirement options and financial decisions.

If you've taken the time to read this book and consider your future, I applaud you because you've taken the time to better educate yourself on what, without adequate coaching, is a very complex subject where there are no second chances. Making the right decisions could be the difference of hundreds of thousands of dollars or even more over your lifetime.

Equally important, this planning gives you the confidence and clarity that because you have taken the time to get your financial ducks in a row, things are going to be all right not just now but in the future. It can take a weight off your shoulders that truly is liberating.

If you're married, then it's important to time travel into the future to discover what's going to happen when your partner passes away, say, in his or her early eighties. How does that look for the survivor?

Unfortunately, ladies, we now know that 90 percent of the time that is you.

If your future doesn't look good when your partner passes away, then that's okay because we are not in the future. You can make changes now to make sure you're taken care of and are able to do all the things that you planned to do for the rest of your life.

The main thing I can't help with is procrastination. You must decide to take the first step. That is truly the hardest step. With so much on the line, the sooner you start planning, the better.

Fear is often a reason behind procrastination, but it should not be. Typically, education can greatly reduce fear. Make sure to ask the questions that are keeping you awake at night.

I assure you that there truly are no stupid questions in retirement planning. There are only regrets for not asking those questions. There is no reason to be afraid or bury your head in the sand. All that does is make it harder to breathe.

We've all had times where we've had regrets. We've known what we should have done but felt things were too hard or embarrassing. Or maybe we thought we simply were too busy.

I remember in the early '80s, I went out on my own and formed an independent business with a guy who was a marketing genius. He introduced me to a little white box, an early version of a particular company's computer that had a piece of fruit for a logo.

I had a chance to buy stock in that company.

But, no, I passed up buying Apple early because I didn't fully understand it.

When it comes to planning for your retirement and maintaining your retirement, you can't afford regrets. That's where a financial advisor can help you capitalize on opportunities. I can help you fully understand what you need to do and when you need to do it.

With my team's help, you can forge ahead with the four basic steps of retirement planning. When we are done creating your plan, particularly your written income plan, I'm betting you will agree the process wasn't hard or overly time-consuming. You'll realize you simply needed to take a bit of time to plan for a lifetime of comfort.

To refresh your memory from the first chapter: We start with a simple conversation where we get to know you, your needs, your goals, your personal culture, and your dreams. This is the discovery meeting.

If we think we can add a lot of value to your life, next we review your current plan. Finally, if you want our help, we spend as much time as necessary using our knowledge and experience to fine-tune your plan so you can retire and stay retired and do all the things you've always wanted to do.

That could be spending more time with your children and grandchildren, improving your golf game (I've been a practicing golfer for more than thirty years), traveling to places you've always wanted to go, maybe buying an RV or boat, spending time at the beach, reading a book, or just doing nothing.

For those of you who are trying to make the best decision, let me try to make it simple with a golf analogy that even nongolfers can understand.

Let's say a golfer had an opportunity to receive the best set of golf clubs money could buy or have ten free lessons from golf great Tiger Woods. Which one should the golfer choose?

The answer is the free lessons because it's not clubs that make a great game. It's technique.

You should spend time educating yourself as much as possible, which includes finding the best coach to help you.

That coach can walk you through the complexities of investing, retirement, taxes, and Social Security among other things, so that you're able to come up with the best strategies for you and your family. Sometimes the coach is just there to listen when you're concerned or afraid.

Over more than four decades, I've helped thousands of people retire and maintain their standards of living for as long as they lived. It would be an honor if you were to entrust me to help you, too.

I'm looking forward to helping you live confidently today, unburdened by worry for the future. I want to help you retire, stay retired, and do all the things you've sacrificed for through the years.

Just give me a call.

My best to you and your family,

~ Brad

About Our Firm: Vineyard Financial

I am often asked how Vineyard Financial's name came to be. I have been in the financial services industry a very long time. I ran my own proprietorship called Ford and Associates beginning in 1981. However, as part of a lawsuit mentioned below, it could only be documented that Ford and Associates had been used with respect to *financial planning* since at least 1988. Prior to 1988, Ford and Associates primarily offered life and health insurance strategies and not financial planning services

Ford Financial Associates filed for registration of the name, Ford Financial Associates" and its design for financial planning services on September 8, 1998, with the first date of use as August 1, 1998, and had used its domain name since August 1998.

Okay, stay with me. I promise this gets more interesting as we go, and these facts make it much more interesting.

Yes, this is building up to a major lawsuit! Can you guess who sued Ford Financial Associates? Well, I can give you a little hint: my dad was named Henry Ford.

On January 1, 2000, Ford Motor Company (FFC) sued Ford Financial Associates (FFA). David versus Goliath! That's the date on the filing complaint for trademark infringement, dilution, and unfair competition. While I can't go into any major details due to the settlement of this lawsuit, I can certainly tell you how it took place, and how this involved one of my dearest old friends.

A friend of mine and I graduated from Harrison High School in 1976. We remain close friends to this day, and I started helping her with her investments and insurance in the late 1980s. We were meeting in my office in January 2000, when I heard the back door alarm go off. I left my private office, went to the back door, and a gentleman said "the back door" was unlocked and gave me a package. I opened the package, and it was a summons from Ford Motor Company versus Ford Financial Associates, Inc.

I briefly read through the document and pretty much had an OMG moment. I'm not saying that I passed out or anything, but since I knew the document was real. I was a little shaken up. I went to my conference room and my friend told me I didn't look good. "Is everything okay?" she asked. I handed her the document, she briefly read it, and said, "I think you need a drink."

Well, the document was very real, and I was blessed by a lot of help from a lot of people, and in particular my insurance company policy that stated it would provide coverage for me with no deductible with an unlimited payout. I immediately hired a legal firm from Detroit, and the game was on.

I won't bore you with the details, although if you'd like to discuss this further, give me a call. There were approximately seven counts (claims) against me, and the financial penalties could be quite substantial.

I remember the judge appointed to this case telling one of my attorneys that they are not going to allow this to be David versus Goliath. Consequently, we were directed to go through mediation first rather than carrying this thing on for years to go to court.

I can only tell you that, in all honesty, the mediation was fun. I had great representation, and we felt strongly that we would win five of the claims against me, primarily due to the incredible legal team that represented me, some work on my part, and a whole lotta work on God's part.

We were down to some final arguments at the end of the mediation, and I mean at the very end of the mediation. I remember stating to the Ford Motor Company attorneys that if they did not agree to this one offer by 10 a.m. tomorrow CST, we would go to court, and I would look forward to going to court. At 9:59 a.m. CST, Ford Motor Company called my attorney and accepted the offer.

Okay, Brad. Who cares about all this stuff and what does this have to do with Vineyard Financial?

As part of the mediation process, I really had no problem giving up the name, Ford Financial Associates. I had always wanted a company that wasn't just in my name, but that portrayed a firm where no one was responsible for everything. I also wanted a name that was Christian-based but not overpowering, and one that I could trademark.

So, once I received this substantial settlement, some said it was one of the largest ever that was not automotive related, and I promise you it would not have paid my mortgage for the year. I instructed my trademark attorney, who had worked with me through this process, to develop a Christian-based name that we could trademark so I would never have to go through this again.

Kathy and I chose Vineyard Financial. Now it is true, my beautiful bride Kathy and I are wine aficionados, so many people think that Vineyard means wine, but it does not. Vineyards are mentioned throughout the Bible; to me, vineyards are places where growth occurs. Through intense pruning, and harvesting, growth takes place at just the right time. If you want more details, I would love to hop on a phone call!

So, there you have it. That's how Vineyard Financial, Inc. was created! You can visit the vineyardfinancial.com website to view the logo.

Hopefully, you've enjoyed the book and took lots of notes. I also hope that it prompted you to make a list of the dreams that you and your spouse or significant other have always wanted to achieve, and have found a way to make them a reality.

Acknowledgments

With more than four decades in this business, it is impossible to thank everyone who has had meaning in my life, yet I feel compelled to mention a few.

I want to thank God and my Savior Jesus Christ for leading and guiding me through the good times and bad, always encouraging me to be better, helping me learn from my mistakes and showing me the real meaning of unconditional love.

They say behind every successful man is his wife. I can only imagine what it would have been like over the last four decades without my beautiful bride, Kathy, by my side. Kathy is always supportive, honest, and loving. She's willing to tell me the truth when I really don't want to hear it, reminds me that others should come first, and helps me remember why I'm in this business. Significantly, Kathy has allowed me time to build the business to the level it is now. She has been an unrelenting source of wisdom to me and a phenomenal mother and mentor to our children.

I also want to thank and acknowledge our four children for being patient with me during their lifetimes as the business often limited my time with them. I've done my best over the last fifteen years to be much more intentional in balancing my time in the business and time with my family.

My parents were unfailingly there for me, giving me direction, love, and the confidence of knowing I could always talk to them no matter what was going on in my life.

I've had several business partners over my career, but Frank Forbes stands out as one who especially helped me grow. When it came time to part ways, as my direction was different than his, we were able to do so in a professional and caring way. We remain friends to this day.

They say iron sharpens iron, and I believe that to be true. I've been blessed with good mentors and accountability partners along the way. Terry Courter, the Rev. Troy Boulware, Bob Jones, Jim and Cheryl Peterson, and so many others were there to provide advice, keep me on track, and help me focus on what was the most important thing in my life.

The friends I have met through this business are almost too numerous to count. My time with Asset Marketing Systems was some of the best of my career — such great mentors and friends. I was blessed to be in a small study group that truly changed my business life. Thank you, Dave Scranton, for inviting me into your group.

I'm also extremely grateful for my relationship with Advisors Excel, which has been transformative in helping me create a balance between my business and personal life. In particular, Christina Gilbert has helped coach me through some of the most difficult times and helped me with my business management. Jeremiah Lauts helped with personal development.

In addition to making my life easier, my Advisors Excel coaches helped me create a strong Vineyard Financial team — one of the best I've had in my four-decade career. I'm especially thankful for my Vineyard leadership team for helping me make important recent decisions.

I also appreciate help from Advisors Excel with my "Refining Retirement" radio show and am thankful for the team's patience and guidance as I've written this book.

Finally, I thank my clients over the years for entrusting me to help you achieve the goals and dreams you so truly deserve.

About the Author

BRAD FORD
President, Vineyard Financial

Brad has a long history of helping clients in or nearing retirement create plans designed to accumulate, protect, and preserve their wealth.

As the leader of his firm, Brad leverages his knowledge and experience to create personalized financial strategies that address the unique needs and challenges that could arise in retirement.

Brad is a Registered Representative and Investment Adviser Representative of Madison Avenue Securities, LLC (MAS), member FINRA/SIPC, and a registered investment advisor. He attended Western Kentucky University and the University of Southern Indiana.

Brad lives in Evansville, Indiana, with his wife, Kathy. Together, they have four children.

In his free time, Brad likes to spend time with friends and family and spoil his seven grandchildren.

MAIN OFFICE
20 NW 3rd Street, Suite 300
Evansville, Indiana 47708

OFFICE OF CONVENIENCE
10475 Crosspoint Blvd, Suite 250
Indianapolis, Indiana 46256

Phone: 812.474.6200
Email: brad@vineyardfinancial.com

Access the link to visit vineyardfinancial.com

www.ingramcontent.com/pod-product-compliance
Lightning Source LLC
Chambersburg PA
CBHW071456220526
45472CB00003B/825